POSITIVELY ME SPIRIT AND I

Aubrey Welch

BALBOA.PRESS
A DIVISION OF HAY HOUSE

Balboa Press books may be ordered through booksellers or by contacting:

Balboa Press
A Division of Hay House
1663 Liberty Drive
Bloomington, IN 47403
www.balboapress.co.uk
UK TFN: 0800 0148647 (Toll Free inside the UK)
UK Local: (02) 0369 56325 (+44 20 3695 6325 from outside the UK)

Because of the dynamic nature of the Internet, any web addresses or links contained in this book may have changed since publication and may no longer be valid. The views expressed in this work are solely those of the author and do not necessarily reflect the views of the publisher, and the publisher hereby disclaims any responsibility for them.

The author of this book does not dispense medical advice or prescribe the use of any technique as a form of treatment for physical, emotional, or medical problems without the advice of a physician, either directly or indirectly. The intent of the author is only to offer information of a general nature to help you in your quest for emotional and spiritual well-being. In the event you use any of the information in this book for yourself, which is your constitutional right, the author and the publisher assume no responsibility for your actions.

Any people depicted in stock imagery provided by Getty Images are models, and such images are being used for illustrative purposes only. Certain stock imagery © Getty Images.

Print information available on the last page.

ISBN: 978-1-9822-8529-6 (sc)
ISBN: 978-1-9822-8528-9 (hc)
ISBN: 978-1-9822-8530-2 (e)

Balboa Press rev. date: 03/01/2022

Dedication

I would like to dedicate this book not only to my children and my grandchildren, but to all of you who are children of the Universe. We all live our lives here and experience the wonder of life, the difficulties and sufferings that it presents not only within this life, but from those past and future lives.

Foreword

The following words were by my friend *Yvette Monroe's* late father and are on her kitchen wall. They may very well have been the starting point for my thoughts, with his words helping to shape and guide me on my journey in writing this book. They appear with her permission.

When we were young
I tried to tell you this
That you were lent not given
And would leave with just a kiss
Go love and live with kindness
And stand against them all
That what us right I bless
But if it is wrong you fall.

This universe belongs to you
Each and every part
So, use it well, see it through
Live it with your heart
For each day a blessing
God given, in a love for all
If mean in thought you are missing
The meaning it of it all
By *Leonard Albert Fillery (April 2003)*

Introduction

Writing a book is something that I have thought about long and hard for many years, and this is my endeavour to shine some light into the uncertainty within the World caused by the COVID-19 Pandemic, to supply encouragement, help, advice, inspiration and ease the darkness which has existed, since that time.

I can most definitely say that I am not an expert. I was never fortunate enough to attend University or study psychology. Life experiences have brought me to where I am now. My knowledge having accumulated over the course of my lifetime. Events and situations, shaping my personal development along the way. After many years of personal difficulty realised that my life purpose is one of healing and helping.

What follows has come from my own thoughts and intention to engender some positivity, happiness, knowledge, helpfulness and general encouragement, to help during these unsettling times, within which we have been living.

You could read the book from cover to cover, but the intention and my concept is for you is too just think on one aspect, one day at a time, and then to open the book randomly, or to a specific page number that comes to your mind.

What you read will then aid and hopefully supply due guidance for you at that moment. This can happen as often as needed, daily, weekly, or whenever the necessity arises.

I hope that this helps with future focus, advice and brings some help and guidance where needed, and encouragement.

"From my heart to yours, I'd like to thank each one of you for being the amazing, courageous souls that you are. Life can be so tough, but you get through it day after day with a smile."

Aubrey Welch

We all have those moments when we feel we would rather not. It is at these times when you can show how amazing you are. You find within yourself something extra, to manage the situation, and to stay stronger and more resilient than you thought you ever thought that you could. The depth of character you have runs so much further than skin deep. It runs there, inbuilt within you and within your soul. Never become disillusioned with yourself. You are amazing. Never think or let anyone tell you otherwise. Life is about happiness, your happiness. Just appreciate who you are. You are precisely where you are for now. Shine your light and weave your magic. The magic which is you and always will be you.

Remember to live love and laugh
To be happy as life is short
Enjoy the plans you make
Experience as much of the world as you can
Allow opportunities to come
They will appear as intended
Let your life occur at the right speed
Everything in its own time and place
If you are too eager, you may miss them
There are opportunities always waiting
You will never know what is just around the corner
Have that I am ready sense of anticipation
Accept to expect the unexpected
The unexpected may just be what you are expecting
It may be the blessing you have longed for.

We live within a world of constant change uncertainty worries and concerns, which can cause us all issues in so many ways. All we can do is look after our own individual situations and try to figure out the best choices and actions which we must make. Although everything we experience, both directly or indirectly, has a connection, it is our own choices and actions which affect us most. We need to let go of that which no longer serves and look for alternative and more beneficial options to take us to the next stage. The next step of our development, and the change which is forever occurring. We may feel hesitant and anxious, that is natural, but staying true to our ideals will enable us to overcome any doubts.

All we can ever be is true to ourselves

Be who we are and to look for and seek goodness

Beauty and love like gloves go hand in hand

See it be it experience it live it

Life is a multifaceted and complex

Which we will never fully understand

That does not matter, just allow

Experiencing good and bad

Helps us to learn and grow

Never experiencing the same twice

The rough with the smooth

Enjoy it live it love it

But whatever, wherever and whenever

Do just be you

An amazing spiritual being who exists in human form for now.

Occasionally, we sense what is coming and get that feeling deep inside. A feeling of either uncertainty, wariness, or even that knowing that yes, this is going to be good. Instinct and that inner reaction count for far more than you would expect. You know that sometimes that something is going to be the only sensible choice to take forward. Trusting in yourself to guide you to where you need to be. Keeping all aspects of yourself fit and healthy is necessary. Exercise, diet, ample relaxation and mediation are vitally important, to achieve a full balance of Mind, Body and Spirit. All parts of you, when balanced, work together in tandem for your benefit and to your advantage. Keep to this simple philosophy and enjoy a more satisfying, happier, and fulfilling life.

The body comes with nothing and leaves with nothing
What happens is what we call it life
We come and go like the seasons
All we really get to experience during it is time
But what is time?
We cannot hold it or capture it
Either we use it, or lose it
It flows and so easily slips away
It is just a measurement for us to manage
In the universal ocean of sky and space
It appears endless and abundant
Was there a time before the start of time?
Will there become a time when time ends
We cannot answer either with conviction
As we just need to make the most of the time, we get
The older we get, the more wisely we accept
Once we understand this concept, the rest potentially falls into place.

Yes, there will be plans, things to do, people to see, but as always, ensure to show kindness, care and compassion not just to one another, but to ourselves as well. Just do not give yourself any hardship about any specific situation which is beyond your control. Just listen to yourself, take your own daily advice, and accept that which will be. Look after yourself, and care equally for all others. Remember to give and you shall receive. You are so important. Remember this because if you do not, then sadly, there may be no one else who will. Make sure you take time for yourself; it is vital that you listen to your body. If you need to find time to do nothing, find time to do exactly that. Doing nothing could be the answer that you need at that specific time.

Every day has a period of darkness and light

The severe storms will eventually pass

Every sun rise is a new opportunity

Take the good with the bad

Accept that your thoughts can affect your mood

Realise that every rainbow cannot have a pot of gold

One day, who knows, keep looking.

Keep wishing on a star all the stars

Stay focused and positive

Enjoy life with care and kindness

Live each day with a purpose

Accept each as if there is no tomorrow

Be powerful and show your strength

Stay focused and believe in your ability

Be yourself always.

To last the journey, we must learn to be patient. We need to live in the current moment, not the past, and realise that the destination is likely unknown. It's not like boarding a train, knowing what time you will leave, and where the scheduled termination point is. We cannot figure out where we will stop, or when the ride of our life will conclude. We just need to accept the changes which lie ahead and make allowances for the many diversions and delays which will occur. Just have complete faith and trust, and imagine each day as being calling points along the way. Yes, there will be many each year, and in total many more than you can imagine. The journey is always forward, and it is your journey to enjoy. Although you will have others go along with you, some for only one stop or two, others many more, it is you and you alone that decide the route you take.

Our dream time is our own time to be free

To go where we meant to go without thought or reason

To see places and meet people we may know

Or more likely those that we don't

Time, whilst dreaming, will seem to last forever

Whilst in our normal time concept, it will only last barely minutes

Which is the wonder of travelling out of body

Going to dimensions beyond our concept of time and space

Each night we do not know where we will go

The wonder of sleep is that it will happen

We go where we go

Meet who we meet

Experience what is going to help

Enabling us to develop within our subconscious state

Bringing us dimensions beyond our control and concept

Get ready to step through the doorway

Tonight, your adventures again await.

Something happens which enables you to uncover and discover the real you, and to find something fundamental and different from yourself that you never knew existed. This will have always been there within, just waiting for the right moment, within your journey, for it to become clear. Reflection and the choices we make allow these hidden doors to appear, and your journey allows you to find the real you. We are all here for a reason, and to learn many lessons along the way. In times of quiet, listen to yourself. You will hear things spoken to you. They will help to guide you forward, and onwards within your journey, allow this information to come to you. It is for you, and only you.

Always be the light
Let others see you share your light
Let it shine out
Show who you are
Let your light be a guide
They will follow the path you tread
Let them walk with you
As you are an example
You are exactly who you are
Never doubt yourself
Never worry about being different
We cannot all be the same
Different thoughts and distinct skill sets
Being different is a bonus
Just be yourself
You are good enough
Be amazing illuminate and shine
We all have it inside
Do not hide this away.

Each day, you wake up with eagerness and anticipation of new possibilities and what the new day will bring. We all see the World in our own individual way. It can never just be black and white. It has many layers and sides, which affect us all differently. The one abounding element which is always there and is all around us all is LOVE. See it. Feel it. Be it. Share it. Let it be the driving force of your life. It is abundant, powerful, completely magical. Not just today, not even just tomorrow. Every day, and then for always and forevermore. There is nothing better to be shared, so experience the wonder of it always and forever.

Our darkest moments are when we need the greatest help

That darkness is so deep and impenetrably dark

The darkest of nights simply does not compare

Always be there for those who need help

Be their sun, their moon and their guiding stars

Help them when they need you

One day, the tables could so easily turn

You may need them to be there for you more than you'd ever know

It may happen so unexpectedly that all you can do is panic for help

Never knowing when it will or could occur

Just be aware that anything can happen

What we give, we get back

Always give first without question

Give loving care and kindness

Receive gratefully and graciously in return.

If we found that life was easier than it is, we would never learn or develop. Part of our development and journey involves us all being constantly tested, stretched, and nudged. Taking us towards the limit of our own individual boundaries, although the limit is endless, we are all on differing journeys. Every opportunity is a new challenge, a new start, an alternative route within our path. The easiest direction may not necessarily be the most direct and may not give us the opportunity to seek the greater level of knowledge needed to take us forwards. Always find that opportunity to quieten the mind, allow yourself this practice often, and to hear that which you need to hear. Meditation is vital to your well-being. Make notes afterwards. Eventually, you will find out more about yourself than you could ever imagine.

Light and dark

Day and night

Yes and no

Good and bad

They are all technically the same

Equal parts and opposites

Two halves making up the whole

Without one, we could not have the other

Everything needs to be balanced

Without which the equilibrium is out of alignment

Life needs continual balance

Keep this in mind always

Endeavour to match it within your life

Giving and receiving are of equal importance

The Universal Law of balance needs respect.

Life can so easily take us off track, and at some stage, we have that sense of feeling lost. It is at these times that we may need to find help or ask for guidance. It is part of the continual process which helps us to grow spiritually, and to move forwards. We all develop differently, from person to person. There is no set guideline. With guidance, nurturing, and allowing ourselves to become more open, we will get there. The journey needs time. It cannot be rushed. Allow it all to unfold, to happen as and when it is. We are all here for a specific reason, and a purpose that can become clear at an early stage of our lives, or we may need to wait until much later in life. We do not decide the timing. Whilst this all occurs; ensure you enjoy and live life to its fullest each day. Never forget that you are here to experience life.

Each pebble was once part of something far bigger
The constant tides over time have changed them
They are now different, rounded and more beautiful
As time passes, it changes us all
We become more rounded
Our true beauty unfolds
Hidden beauty which was always there
We are born with it within
When ready, we too change
It becomes our enduring light
We then illuminate and we shine
So, when you are ready to change
Allow the process to happen
It will be part of your journey
Shine bright shine strong
Like a searchlight in the sky at night
Helping those in greater need than you.

We are all visitors, and like all, tourists cannot stay in one place forever or overstay our welcome. Travelling through the many dimensions of time and space, our journey is long. We have many varied lives and experience different places of existence along the way. The Universe has no bounds, no limits, and our souls likewise. What we learn helps us within that life journey, but we may remember nothing beneficial from each stage to help our development along the way. We are but a spirit within a shell, a shell that serves as our home, and serves us well until it is our time to move on, and our transition takes us onwards.

Darkness and Light

Sun and Moon

Yin and Yang

Nature or Nurture

Good and Bad

Right or Wrong

Yes or No

Do and Don't

Stop and Go

Heads or Tails

There are always two sides to the coin

Life is the same

The answer to everything is

Balance and Harmony

Imbalance and Chaos

We are the controllers

The catalysts of our lives

Decide where, how, why and when

Alternatively, leave it all to Chance.

It is never easy to find our inner or our outer balance. Each day is different, but with careful thought, planning and desire, this is achievable. Find time to yourself, time to meditate and quieten your mind. Go deep within, into your own personal private sanctum. Listen to what occurs, contact will come from your guides, your spirits, your ancestors, and your angels who all constantly surround you. Set aside time each day for this exercise, and gradually you will become more aware of who you really are. It is an ongoing life process, enabling you to find peace, reflection and so much more besides. Always be grateful for what you learn. The advice that comes may not make immediate sense, but given time, it will become invaluable.

Should we take everything at face value?
Can we believe all we see, hear, or read?
Where should we turn to if we want to check facts and information?
Life is now full of more data than ever before
It is a conundrum of duplicity
The bias is so often misleading
Never the same advice from different sources
We must try to judge it all
Gather and assimilate the facts
Make up our own minds
Not allowing yourself to be controlled
To ensure that free will prevails
It is not as easy as it sounds
Nothing ever is straight forward.

What we say or do is because of our own thoughts and reality. So always ensure that you are kind, caring, and considerate. What we hear others say, or what they do, is due to theirs. Although we should all be the same and live a spiritual life, sadly, that is not the case. Rise above the negativity of comments and situations. Allow your natural inner strength and positivity to see you through. Being able to stay strong in all situations, especially those that test your strength of character, is a wonderful way to be. Staying strong doesn't mean being over dominant, just showing that you are mentally tough, with sound stability. Understanding that situations can easily run out of control, and a minor issue can twist into a major problem. Stay calm, collected, but importantly, in control of all situations.

We all can heal and be healers
A natural gift and ability within each of us
We need to trust ourselves more
Helping others also helps us to help ourselves
It helps us to heal that inner hurt we carry
Have faith and truly believe in this gift
That it is possible and can happen
Have faith in yourself
Have faith in your own ability
We are all part of the same universe
It is within every one of us
The doorway to this opens from life's experiences
It enables us to help others freely
In time, it will enable them to help others back
Helping them mentally emotionally spiritually physically
Helping should be like breathing
Automatic and without thought.

We are all on a journey which was predestined and started the second we were born. We did not know then where life would take us or where we would go or what we would experience to reach this current point. It will have taken us in many and varying directions. Many crossroads will have occurred, and we are now at a major juncture and impasse. This is giving us all the opportunity to re-evaluate the journey we have had and where we would like to go next. During your dream time, all these opportunities, past, present and future, will play out, giving you unexpected insight and knowledge. From this, you will either consciously or subconsciously guide forward. Remain open to all possibilities and opportunities.

What should we look to hold on to?
What should we decide we need to let go?
There is a fine line between the two
There is no definitive answer
Making the right choice is never easy
Making sure it is a well thought out plan
Acting quickly can cause regret
Act too slowly and other factors can become increasingly important
Neither choice is ever easy to say or to do
Neither possibility is far from straight forward
Holding on needs strength and the need for bravery
Letting go possibly requires even more strength and fortitude
We just must try to make the best choice we can and at the time
We afterwards live with what we have decided
Decisions are what life really is all about
Many started before birth
All decisions are for a reason and at specific time
All decisions, right or wrong, are part of your path
They are part of you.

There are some people who will never listen, never understand what you are trying to say. They only focus on their own thoughts, and their way of life, making them oblivious to the views other than their own. All they want to do is to be in control, and to enforce control over all others, and if they can make you more like them. Fortunately, we all have free will, and can take own decisions. Our own frequency will usually feel more attuned to those of a similar mindset and way of life. Hold on to your beliefs and values. Let those seeds within nurture your thoughts, your actions, and, in time, sprout into ideas. Those ideas can then turn into becoming reality, your reality. There is an inexhaustible supply of seeds, so restarting the process is a never-ending cycle, like life itself.

I wrote a letter to the Universe
It wasn't for posting
Instead, I tied it to a balloon
Let the wind decide where to take it
Like, a note in a bottle drifting at sea
I watched it float on the wind
Higher and higher until it was soon out of sight
Will there ever be a response?
I cannot say for sure
Sometimes we just must allow
To go with the flow
See where life takes us
Allowing those thoughts to fly
Trusting believing in the process
It is worth taking a chance
I can always try again
Never think of giving up
Life is an adventure
Each journey is a lesson.

We are most definitely within a world of chaos, with uncertainty is everywhere. It often seems that we a supplied with an overload of information and statistics daily. We just need to look beyond the obvious. See and appreciate that life can be beautiful. There are still so many good things to appreciate. The birds in the trees, singing at dawn or dusk. Our sun high in the sky each day. The trees, plants, and flowers awakening then growing after their winter hibernation. The stars in the sky, and the planet which is our home. If we step back and take a divorced view, we will see, feel and appreciate that what we have is something truly wonderful.

When we listen properly, we really listen

We are utterly and completely silent

We pay compete attention

No interrupting or loss of interest halfway through

No wondering what is happening elsewhere

We listen and take in that which we are being told

We can then consider the situation

We may not know the exact answers or options

But we can advise, and we can try to help

But first, we must listen in silence

Unless we do that, the conversation becomes wasteful

It is never easy, but it is achievable

Listen and Silent have the same letters

Because they serve the one purpose.

What today will bring, we cannot say. We will go about my usual business quietly watching, listening and with patience. We take in what is happening, although it may not all at once show that we know what is going on. This is who we are. There is not much that we miss. We allow ourselves time to collect, then assimilate the information. We can then take any necessary action. We will always be protectors of those dear to our hearts, and that is how it will always be. Being there for them all, even when we cannot be there with them personally. We need to be always ready to make a move and to help without hesitation. So just be aware that the moment to help may come.

You need to dance to your own tune
No one else knows exactly your thoughts
No one else knows exactly your mood
They may have an idea
They may be highly intuitive
But they will never be completely correct
So go on, let your music play
That music deep down inside
Which is there just waiting
Follow your beat
The rhythmic beat of your heart
The spiritual beat of your soul
Let it all take you to where you want to be
It's there waiting for you
So come on strike a chord
Dance the day
Dance the night away
You can dance to your tune
You have a tune within your essence.
The tune of your beauty
The tune of you are and your amazing life.

It is the start of a new day. Forget what happened yesterday, forget even what happened last week and start again with a blank page ready for filling. It is yours to fill it with whatever you need. At this stage, you may not clearly understand, but just allow yourself, when necessary, to be guided. Allow the opportunity to show you the way. All those times when things have not gone right have opened as your own personal cracks, making you feel slightly broken, but they have let light in. The light has enabled you to become who you are at this very moment. You are amazing and you are enough as you are. So, why change? Just stay being who you are. Go on, show who you are. Inspire dazzle and feel the magic that is there within. Remember, just be you.

It is a completely unique encounter

A connection so strong

Linking hearts without bounds

Bridging the gap between two

Such a bond firmly joined

It will take you completely by surprise

Capturing your essence

Way beyond just trust

Nothing else is like it

It is like a drug but so pure

Yes, addictive, but in a good way

Fill up with it regularly

It eases the aches

Takes away the pains

Makes you think about tomorrow

Leaves yesterday behind

Soothes the mind

Heals the body

Resuscitates the heart

Re-enforces the soul

It is a pure essence

Love is everything.

When we get knocked down; we think how we shall start again. How we act and how we react makes all the difference. Do we reflect, regroup, brush ourselves off, show our resilience, our resolve and then get right back up again? After a period of reflection, and an opportunity to rethink, of course we do. We do not show defeat in any shape or form. We show that we have more inner strength than anyone could ever expect. We reappear even stronger than we ever were before. The more this happens, the more we end up learning about ourselves. It would be so easy to go along a route allowing ourselves to enter a dark, endless tunnel from which we may never reappear. So never think that a setback is the end. Think of it as stopping off point along the journey, which is your life. All those stopping off points happen for a reason. Embrace them all, every one. Do not be afraid of them. They are part of your development.

Taking that first big step
That giant leap of faith
It can be nerve-wracking
You may have prepared thoroughly
You may feel totally ready
Until you decide to say yes
Then self-doubt appears
The what ifs, the whys and wherefores
That is when faith steps in and takes over
Your faith in yourself and who you are
In your abilities, proven or otherwise
Trust and faith in the Universe
So just believe that you are ready
It may not go smoothly
There may be a glitch or two, and setbacks
Life would not be life if it was all plain sailing
But first you need to take that first step
You know that will be only the start
Give yourself due time and effort
The reward in the long-term will be worthwhile
It is a journey of wonder and discovery.

Communication is such an important part of our lives. Not only how we perceive communication with others, so we do not end up with presumptions but also how we communicate with ourselves. It is essential that we spot all the signs. They are so easily missed. Once communication wanes, then sadly other aspects will follow, a downward trend occurs. This potentially leads to the end of relationships and friendships. We therefore need to pay more attention to this in all aspects of our daily lives. Our main communication with ourselves is, of course, non-verbal and mainly through our own intuitive feelings. These are easily miserable, so be alert and ready, because they may not immediately jump out and say anything. It takes time and practice to how know these feelings affect your life. Learn to understand them. They will be beneficial.

Like a conductor with a batten
We orchestrate our own lives
The world helps us to play out our symphony
Forever flowing, forever showing
Music so delicate, spiritual and pure
It lightens and brightens up our lives
The wonder is way beyond imagination
Sit back, connect and enjoy your own show
It is your show, yours alone, to enjoy
It is the heartbeat and rhythm of your life
It is your own inner tune from the universe
So go on, get set and raise that batten
Lift it high when ready
Let your music play
Feel your life reverberate to your tune.

Are you always looking to learn, to increase your knowledge, and do you think of yourself like that of a wise old owl? Or even your very own oracle, with a depth of information, who certainly knows a thing or two about life, and how to be living your best life. We all like to watch, wait, listen, and keep alert and ready. It is something that we can all do, and it does not even need special skills, or really any major practice. Just take time to sit in silence and to be quiet. It is amazing what you will hear, feel, or sense in those moments of silence. There is so much we can learn, and which we need to learn; it is part of the journey of life. Try it today, time allowing. Let those moments of reflective solitude help you shape and take hold of your life, moving it forward and in an amazingly different and new direction.

Which path should we choose?

There are so many varying options

If it is not our path, then possible one that others wish

There is no definitive correct choice

The ones you choose are the ones for you

We may often wonder where and why

Are we going in the right direction?

It is within us but ultimately beyond our full control

We just must go with what feels right

It will eventually lead us in the right direction

Like a labyrinth with its many twists and turns

Only one way in and one way out

It is a journey of discovery

Discovering your true self

It is a long road spanning this and many lifetimes

Just accept it and take it step by step

Take the journey of your lifetime

In the end, you will discover who you truly are.

Always try to watch out for synchronistic coincidences in your every day-to-day life, because they are all around. Some will be easy to spot and more noticeable than others. They are all equally important, matter to us all differently, so endeavour to see them, listen out for them, and to find as many as you can. They will be there every day, but not always easily noticeable. It's a bit like putting a puzzle together without an illustration to guide us finding and then fitting all the segments together. Some pieces will be so much easier than others, but they will be there. Ask your own guides for a sign. They will never disappoint. They will want to help. Remember, the first piece starts the process, and then there will be many others to supplement those in time, enabling you to move your journey onwards. Those signs and pieces will not be the same for each of us as our journeys differ. Remember that what applies to you is important for you, so make sure that you take note.

Do we have full resolve?
Can we be completely resolute?
Do we believe and have faith?
That we can trust in the process
That we can live in harmony
Not just with ourselves
But with all others
That we can live a truly valued life
Live life as you agree with your universal decree
Hopefully, it will be a perfect life
Life is never perfect, but we make what it is
It is a mixed bag, including of good luck
Work ethic, effort, and fortuitousness
So, make the most of who you are
Make the most of the skills you have
Learn news ones, open new doors
Accept where you are in life
Be who you are and trust the process
You are part of the process
The process is also part of you
It works both ways.

Just because your position in life puts you in a different place to someone else, this does not affect where you are within your spiritual journey. The spiritual journey is a completely unique path to your human life route, although they do overlap.

Your development enables you to know more about yourself, and the more respect, care, and gratitude you show towards all others, the more you will move along your designated path. So, ensure that you treat all others as you would want them to treat you. Each day, whatever the situation, we all can do something differently to how we may have done it before. To help and to show that we are always growing and learning about life. Life can be more than just okay. So, show the world that you want to stand out for the best possible of reasons. That you are here not just to fit in and become a number. Take that next step and make that happen today. Your future human and spiritual selves will be so proud of you. Make yourself proud, proud of you.

I am

I am me

I am just me

Just as I am, I am enough.

I can

I can try

I can try even harder

Each day, I can try my hardest

I will

I will try

I will try again today

Every day I will keep trying

I can

I can change

Necessity encourages change

I can and will also develop

I will continue to improve

I am, I can, and I will

This will be my foundation for a better life.

It is so easy to look at every issue in life as something complex and difficult to resolve. Try to keep things in balance and as simple as possible. There is never any need to take anything to the extreme. Just focus on one aspect, and one day at a time. What needs doing today needs to happen today, so don't fret about what may happen, or is going to happen tomorrow. Enjoy each day as it comes and goes. We can never tell exactly what is going to happen, so being ready for the unexpected. You do not need to be pushing yourself every single moment. If you cannot find time to explore all your ideas and thoughts, they will just come and go. Genius is doing things with simplicity with ease, and we can therefore all be geniuses in the making. Just be you, let others be themselves. Life is not a competition, so just be concerned with your life. Think like a winner, because whatever others may think, you are one!

Everything is Energy
Everything we think
Everything we do
We always have it with us
We always have it within us
It is the essence of us
It never stops moving
The more we do
The more we need
Use your energy wisely
Keep your energy safe
It is so easily wasted
Your energy speaks volumes about you
Negative energy inhibits negative action
Positive energy radiates a positive mindset
Engendering your light and your love
Be that constant ball of positive energy
Forever growing and glowing brighter
Just be the eternal star which you are.

Are we ready for a new day and whatever it may bring? What we feel with the heart is far more important, more transparent and important than that which we see with our eyes. It is more meaningful, much more in-depth and clearer. It enlivens your inner senses; something that sight alone cannot achieve. To feel it just believe in it, and it will become clearer and more obvious. Life and opportunities come and go, altering our understanding. Acceptance is the key, experiencing major changes and potential wrongs enable the process to start inside. It can often be a very difficult, slow, highly emotional and ongoing process throughout your entire lifetime. Never lose heart. Stay resolute, find your inner courage. Lift your head high, venture out into the world daily with an air of astute and positivity. Never worry about what others may do or think, as we all must decide what is right for us. Just get through each day the best that you can. No one else is you, and all you can ever do is try. Be yourself, stay focused always, live your best life.

The meaning of it all
What is the meaning of it all?
Will we ever know the actual answer?
They say if you dream it, then it can become reality
But what if life is just one big dream?
Do we then have control over what happens
Are our lives the question of life
Searching constantly for the answer
Try hard and always analyse
Life is indubitably a conundrum
Circumspect and different for us all
However difficult we get through it
Doing what we can to open the doors meant for us When
expectation occurs, refocus and rethink
Keep your feet firmly on the ground
Find your own safety net
A place of invisible sanctuary
It is there always with you
Reality may not be how we perceive it.

Will we truly ever know the answer to the question of life, why we are here, and the reason for our existence? It is something that could be for continual exploration and discussion. Infinite thoughts throughout eternity, without a defined explanation. We may haphazardly come to our own differing conclusions, which will be our own views. But in all honesty, without a shadow of doubt, we will never know the complete answers. Likewise, do we even ever fully know who we are ourselves? Again, the answers may only be partially in the affirmative. We are always learning something new, something else about who we are. If we had all the answers at the outset, then life would not be the adventure, the test which it is. It is more than an assessment, and unlike an examination, there are not any completely right or wrong answers. The more we think about it, the more there is to ponder, the more there is to discover about the past and those who have been here before us. Considering, discussing, evaluating, forever learning should always be the case. Broadening the mind and advancing thought patterns.

We are all mortal, every one of us
Whatever we may think
In the end, we are here for a set period
None of us is immortal
Longevity may happen for a selective few
Others may not experience the same
We never know the length of the journey
As the time we are each given will differ
We must accept this as fact, not fiction
Likewise, each day is different
Yesterday, today, and then tomorrow
Accept what has been gone and is coming
Today is your present
Yesterday is already the past
Each passing day becomes your history
Live in the moment of the day
Fill the chapter with sensible wise decisions
Leave tomorrow, for tomorrow
That is a completely new page
Each day has their own individual synchronicities
Accept them on their own merits
Live in the here, and in the now.

As a species, we are constantly developing and strengthening as a whole, and not just individually. Events happen, which although not necessarily noticeable speed up the process and then move, us all along the conveyor belt of time. We will eventually be completely different to how we are now and how we appear, but like the development of the butterfly, it cannot happen overnight. This process will never be immediate, and those changes will not be noticeable externally for many millennia. The most important changes will happen first, deep inside. Our development will continually move us onwards, as it has done since the dawn of humankind. In time, we will appreciate all these changes, but for now, all we can do is take each day as a new beginning and a new start. Accept who you are, and try to understand why you are here, how you are part of the universe.

Rain can be such a smoothing sound
Listening to it late at night in bed
The droplets against the windows
Rhythmically, like a metronome
Drop after drop after drop
Lulling your senses into a state of pure relaxation
Freeing you from your own thought processes
Engendering calm and peace
Soon your body will relax fully
A state of deep sleep hopefully awaits
Dreams sitting there already at the cusp of your mind
Adventures awaiting beyond your imagination
Let them take you to wherever they want
The World is where you exist for now
The Universe being your eternal home
Enjoy the splendour of both
It is all connected, as you are too.

Life is all about learning and continuing to grow. This is achievable, but we must always keep asking and questioning. Then, with rational thought and considered sensible analysis, assimilate that which has come to our attention. We will never know everything that just cannot be possible, but if you can learn something new regularly, then that would be wonderful. There is so much that we can learn that we will never know, not just about life and the world, but about ourselves. Before we can find the answers, we need to first search for the questions and clues. They are everywhere but are just not necessarily always easy to spot. Keep looking and do not become despondent. They are waiting for you to look and to find them. Allowing you to make a breakthrough, to appear from what was your darkness into the light. This will help you see your way ahead more clearly, and with your inner wisdom, become an everlasting beacon. A guiding light not just for yourself and your journey, but for all others in need. It may be a slow, arduous process. Have faith and trust you are doing amazingly well. Keep doing this day after day.

When you slow down, you really see life
You come to realise more about what it is
At speed, we overlook so much
It is all far too easily missed
See the beauty of life
Open your eyes
Open your heart
Fill up your senses
Look, become more aware
Search for synchronicities
Many questions will flow
The answers will follow
Clarifying confusion
Finding solutions
Live in the now
Not the past or even tomorrow
One day, one step at a time
Enjoy your journey
Live and love the experience of life
It is your lifetime to live.

Our time is without a doubt short, and our own experience is merely a grain of sand in time. It slips away so quickly and is then gone. The solution is to try not to waste the time you have. Every second, every minute, every hour, and every day counts and is important. Live your life, rather than the potential of losing your life. We are all perfect, beautiful individuals, but none of us are completely flawless. We are all part of the Universe and made from the same materials. Even the most precious diamonds can have their own flaws. They need cutting, shaping, and cleaning before their brilliance may shine. Allow yourself time and effort to shine, too. Just be yourself and be the way you are. We are not perfect; all we can do is look for and endeavour to reach somewhere close to perfection.

Up high in the corner
Minding my business
Doing what I need to do in total silence
I sometimes do nothing
Other times I weave
An intricate patterned detailed elaborate web
My aim is survival, watching and catching my prey
You can so easily take my example of life
It never has to be just be rush, rush, rush
Doing nothing will often take you further
Planning and knowing what you need to do
Why worry about chasing your life all the time
You will never catch what has gone in the past
You just end up going around and around
You may never weave a web
But you can plan how to move from A to B
So, relax, think and make that plan
What I can achieve in a day
Others may take so much longer
But we are on different paths
Accept yours and take it at a pace which suits
The aim of life is development and achievement
Never be afraid to take a chance when opportunity calls.

It may be a new day, or even a new week, each one being different, and may be happy, sad, easy, even tough. Try to get through it the best you can, with a smile and a grateful heart. Stay motivated with a positive mindset in readiness for the opportunities which will appear. There is no point living in the past, or constant worry about what tomorrow may bring. Accept and just take each day as it is, focus on the now and what this moment holds. Have plans, new ideas, and future thoughts, but try never to get so engrossed that the present day passes you completely in a blur. Live for now, and experience and appreciate what that day offers. What you find waiting for you will more than likely amaze you.

What, where or how actually is paradise?
Is it something tangible that we can see sense or touch?
Is it somewhere we can go off to for peace and serenity?
Is it a place we can travel too for the holiday of a lifetime?
Is it something we can only imagine?
We will all have our own interpretation
Each of us will have differing thoughts and ideas
The only authentic place of paradise we all have is within
It is a place that exists there for all of us
We need to journey deep into our inner selves
To block out all the pain
Remove the anguish which life gives
Find somewhere you can truly relax
Finding it will never be easy
But find that place of peace, and of love
Your own place of pure peace and love
With practice, we can achieve this
Keep searching and trying
It is there, you just need patience
Find and enjoy your own piece of paradise.

We cannot change the past, the present is still developing, and going forwards. We can only look at that with the expectation of what is coming, which includes feelings of being so physically and mentally tired. They just float about, and have no set format or pattern. They are with us as a constant, getting us ready for the next stage of our development. Evolution takes forever, but we need to accept that it will always be occurring. The end, if there is a designated end, will be so far ahead and away in time that we will never experience it. There is, of course, a catalyst, and a continual starting point. The future is a gateway slowly opening and taking us forwards. Each new tomorrow is the next onward step, with time and space both potentially being infinitum.

Whatever comes our way, we need to handle it
It is possible that we did not plan it
We may not like it
We likely do not actually want it
Whatever it is, we must accept it
We must then deal with it accordingly
That part of what life is about
Acceptance without judgement
Action without question
Doing without knowing
Guided and believing
Life is such a complex conundrum
Sometimes we all must wonder
We can all think why and how
But do we really want the full answer?
Does it feel better sometimes not knowing?
Accepting that understanding is a facet of life.

Every day is an opportunity for fresh growth, new ideas, the formulation of potential beliefs which can then burst into life. Our thought processes help us nurture our minds, bringing new ways of thinking. We must, therefore, always be open to change, allowing our continual development to occur. Just keep trying as hard as you can, forget about stress and worry, let them go. Be yourself today, tomorrow, and always. You are an amazing individual. Never try being someone else. Give yourself due credit, and just reward, even when things are tough. Some days are tougher than others. They are there to test you; and to test your inner resolve. It enables you to develop who you are and why you are you. Without this, we would never move forward. We would remain unchanging and stagnant, in who we are, and in our beliefs.

We hear her whispers calling
We hear her speaking in the air
Words floating like angels in the wind
Trees constantly speaking out
Clouds float by with their silent tunes
Light plays in the rain
The sea, the oceans grumbling and groaning
Mountains creak and volcanoes roar
The earth herself rumbles deep down inside her core
She is always talking
Telling us we need to be awake and alert
We need to listen
Not to just listen but to realise
From what we see and hear to learn
There is so much we need to learn
Knowledge forgotten over time
Being slowly divulged
Let her music soothe you
Helping with our understanding
Our Mother Earth, our home
She is all knowing and watched over by Father Sky.

Do you know where? Because I do not know where the journey will take us today, what it will bring, or where it will lead us. All I know is that we need to ensure that we make it the best we can and a memorable day. A day which you can look back on in time with more than a smile. Although difficult, endeavour to leave worry and concern, as they only lead to more of the same. Focus on more positive and happier thoughts, on that which you want, not on what you do not. Try your best each day, to be even more positive than before. Yes, even this is difficult, but it will help you raise your personal vibration. When and where you can, put a spin on any areas of negativity, turning it around into positivity. Take each aspect of your daily life separately. Do not get bogged down by taking too many varying options all at once. This, sadly, will not work, as you will quickly lose focus. Aim always to stay focused, positive, forward thinking, and open to the many changes of direction that will occur throughout each day of your life.

The tide was slowly coming in
Gentle waves lapped the shoreline
Across the bay, there was no discernible difference between sea and sky
As we crossed the slowly cooling sand
The last embers of the setting sun glistened on distant water
A sparkly glow of blues, reds and yellows
The air was warm still, and all was completely serene
As the sky darkened, the stars gradually appeared
It was just a perfect night for beach walking
So, few people were about
It was as if we had the world to ourselves
The vastness before us was amazing
The quietness and the developing dark
Wonderfully lost in the experience
Time meant nothing
It was as nothing
All that mattered was the present
Being in the moment
A moment which would last a lifetime
Lifetimes, made better by such moments
The best things in life are free
Love them and enjoy them whilst you can.

So many constantly conflicting choices. Life is full of them each day. They will vary from the mundane to the more decisive, even if sometimes the easiest are the hardest to make. Each choice first considered, then weighed up the best they can, but even then, we may not be totally sure of the route to take. The mind and the heart are not necessarily in balanced agreement. In the end, we all go with whatever possibility feels correct at that moment. Trusting in ourselves and our intuition. Let your feelings, your natural internal guiding compass, show you the way. Your guidance will normally be correct. Listen, feel and trust. Trust in you. You know best. Best for you. Believe sense, feel and then decide. Considered thoughtful, balanced action.

Are you the black sheep of the family?

Do you stand out from the crowd?

Do you find you cannot blend in even though you try?

Do you differ in so many ways to the rest of the flock?

Do you often feel ignored?

Have you even felt bullied for being different

Do you like to learn and to be you alone?

Are you developing into someone that they never can?

Are you trusting in yourself and your intuition?

Have you learnt about survival and how to survive

Have you adapted developed into someone who sees so much more

Yes, every family has one

We are without a doubt the blessed

Yes, we may well be outsiders, oddities, or loners

We stand out because we are just us, and are different

I am happy being me, and who I am

Would I want to change?

Why would I want to change?

Simply categorically and absolutely not

Stay true to yourself, your values and virtues.

Make today the day to put yourself not necessarily first, but on an equally level footing with everyone else. You will naturally be there for family friends, and even strangers, giving them everything that they may need in the way of help, care and kindness. It is now time to do this for yourself, too. This does not mean you have to stop caring about others. That would not go with your own thoughts and philosophy of life. It just means that it is time for self-care, self-love to become more clear, important and obvious. The difference will amaze you, to your life, and to how you feel about yourself. Looking after yourself is vitally important. It is necessary for all aspects of your well-being. Start the process without further delay, because if you do not do this, no one can do it for you. Never think that this is being selfish. It is not the case and never will be.

The meaning of it all
What is the meaning of it all?
Will we ever know the actual answer?
They say if you dream it, then it can become reality
But what if life itself is just one big dream?
Do we then control what happens
Are our lives the question of life
I cannot answer
I can only analyse
Life will always be a conundrum
Circumspect and different for us all
We get through it the best we can
Taking advantage of many opportunities
Doors open when they're meant to
Understanding the difference between acceptance and expectation
Keeping our feet firmly on the ground
Knowing how to find a safety net when needed
Because reality may never actually be how we perceive it
It is how we live it and allow it into our daily lives.

However difficult it can be, we must utilise the time we have to the best of our abilities. Some days are so much tougher, harder, and difficult. Energy levels are low, and a lack of motivation is clearly understandable. It is on days like these we need to push ourselves, to carry out something, anything, however small, that benefits. It is so easy to be wasteful and lose time. Once it is gone, it won't come back and give us a second chance. Every difficult situation makes us want to drift from one day to the next. Try not to let this happen. It can be so hard sometimes to find something useful to do, or even think of looking to learn something new. Never allow boredom to become the norm. It is our dreams which keep us going. They are never all going to come true, so the more dreams you have, the better will be your chances of at least one eventually succeeding. Keep them secret between yourself, your spirits, and your guides. Let them work with you and allow the magic of the Universe to work with you. Just believe in yourself, be open, ready, and accept that the magic you look for is you.

Each night ensure you wipe the slate clean
Leave the thoughts from today behind
Close your eyes imagine a sky bursting full of stars
They are there in an absolute abundance
Of course, you will never see them all
Counting them that would take many lifetimes
Most are many distant light-years away
Going backwards through time
That is when that light left them
So far back we cannot imagine
We see them now
But they may have already have gone
Do not let your life take forever
Live in the here and now
Each day acting, not waiting
We are stars that live here on Earth
Shine your individual brilliance
Illuminate the planet and those you encounter.

Each day of life is part of the ever-continuing lesson from which we never stop learning. We all make mistakes; it is human nature to err. After another occurrence happens, we stop. Before the process repeats, we will have a periodic time of life that goes well. We keep going no matter what has happened before. We look to start again and continue the process. The good with the bad is what we learn to take. Never truly knowing what is coming from one moment, and especially one day to the next. Accepting that this is life and how it is. Keep learning, developing, trying and learning, developing, trying. It is an endless cycle, day after day after day after day. Taking what we can as a positive from each day. Putting any suffering or hurt behind, moving on and allowing ourselves to grow. It is a continual process. Enjoy each day, as they do not come again. Make sure that happiness, care, compassion and love are top of the list for yourself as well as for all others.

Always love yourself and be happy
Give love freely, including yourself
Allow your inner peace to keep you safe from harm
Do not allow yourself to be controlled
Accepting that each day is different on its merits
Sometimes standing still is better than forwards
Going backwards is not an option
Believe in who you are
Even if no one else does
Realise that you are more than simply amazing
You are unshakeable, and unbreakable
Like a rock, you have weathered every storm
Your hard edges having softened over time
What comes tomorrow, however hard?
Cannot and will not break you
Do not second guess situations, or people
Just be proud of who you are
You are fabulously unique
An individual of beauty, strength and character.

Today, and as we should every day, be grateful for so many things that go right in our lives. Be joyful, content, and trust in the wait for what is coming, not just for today but going forwards. Whatever happens beyond yourself, make sure that today is not only a great day, but an easy one. Let all past issues go, to ensure and then not allowing them not to snap back. We must learn to forget, otherwise whatever they are, they constantly prey and become entrenched within our thoughts. Remember that you are better than that, and have the strength to hold all situations, and to move on. It can and will take time to develop and grow, so don't expect instant miracles. Just let them happen as they will within their own time, and at their own speed. Your future happiness depends on this, take expectation away from your thought process, and leave it aside forever.

Decisions are a constant of life

Some happen instantly with no thought

Others take time, are more involved requiring balanced judgement

Either way, they are as they meant to be

We will make good ones, which prove beneficial

Others will not be in your favour

It is all about balance and acceptance

You will win some, you will lose some

The Universe is there supplying help

It can help you part of the way, but not totally

Otherwise, we'd never learn to decide for ourselves

This leaves you to choose which way you finally go

These decisions help us grow and develop

Life is a process, a true learning process

It starts at our beginning and continues verbatim for life.

Appreciation: what is it we appreciate? It may be something that we hardly ever think about, just another word. But if looked at and considered, it means so much more. Especially if considered with the actions that go with it. It then means more than you can easily imagine. It is a sincere thank you, a term of deep-felt gratitude, a true thank you for everything you have. Remember to show this all the time. It's so easy not to even say the simplest thank you, meaning that you naturally expect everything that happens. That ego part of your mind needs to realise, accept, and understand that this just is not the case. Do not allow it to become the norm. Be thankful always, have no misunderstanding, we need to be grateful. So, be truly appreciative each day, no matter however small or large and for whatever the reason, the importance is the gratitude shown.

Is this the beginning of the end?
Or the end of the beginning?
Two totally different conceptual ways
We will all look at this differently
Old ways ending or a fresh new start?
Evaluation of how we are strengthening
The light and the dark
The good and the bad
Right and wrong
Transformations and transmutation
The answers will eventually become clear
Staying resolute because it is always happening
As it has happened many times before
We are spiritual beings living within human form
With the embodiment of life within our souls
We are time travellers and always have been
Our spirit moves onwards to another place and time
An endless journey, an adventure of our lives
Just ensure that you the live your current one.

What stops you from becoming unstoppable? Absolutely nothing does, apart from you. So, get set and raise those thought levels, use today for a springboard of motivation and purpose. However, you feel, get ready for action. Some days it feels easier than others, mind and body not working together in a co-ordinated way. Although we should be ready for action each day, it can occasionally be so difficult. Keep the body, keep the mind and keep yourself active. Try to push yourself that little harder when needed. It may not be easy, you may not feel like it, but just try to do it, because no one else can do it for you. You are ready; you have always been ready, so show everyone that you mean business. Nothing is going to stop you, even if some days it takes longer for that motivation to surface. Set a higher standard, make a difference today, tomorrow, and forevermore!

Anger solves nothing
The problem still exists
It may even have worsened
Situations become strained
Bite your lip
Stamp your feet
Throw a tantrum
But in the end, you will be back where you started
You must learn to see things from both sides
What has happened?
Or may have been said?
We cannot change them
The hands of the time cannot go back
However hard to accept the situation
Move onwards and rise above issues that hurt you
Be magnanimous in your understanding
Just leave the issues with you
Taking them forward will not do you any good
Learn to live, and to let live.

What do we need to remember today? There is so much going on. Remember to be thankful, accept and appreciate that we have another opportunity, another day of life. A new day, and with new challenges. Most will be very similar to yesterday, but they will never be quite the same. Expect the unexpected, visitors arriving out of the blue, or an unplanned conversation. In fact, anything which is unscheduled. We never quite know what may happen. This unpredictability, giving us an exciting aspect to the microcosm life. So, take it just one step at a time, one day at a time. Today is just today. It is not yesterday, and most definitely not tomorrow. Accept what occurs, and when over, look back and consider it good, bad, indifferent, realising that each day is as individual as we are ourselves.

We are all at different spiritual levels
It has nothing to do with who or where you are in life
It relates to your own development
For some, it happens early
For others, it takes their what seems like a lifetime
In the end, we all end up where we are
Being tested and tested, once again
There is no badge or certificate
But you just know that you are on your correct path
Many kinds of devils will have appeared
Each having their own tricky traps
There is no set manual or guide to help
Being drawn to learn that which seems appropriate
In your own way, each of you will have succeeded
You will become your own pupil, teacher and master
The process is constantly in motion
Life is a test, testing your emotions
No one ever suggested that it would be easy
It is difficult, but it is how life is.

What will come your way today? What obstacles will you need to overcome? However, your resolve gets tested. Stay calm and stay in control of yourself and your thoughts. Let your positive energy flow, as the Universe responds accordingly to positivity. Anxiety or sudden panic attacks can and will happen. They are part of life, and something that you may sadly need to deal with unexpectedly. You may feel over eager for so many reasons. You can face problems during any time of day, and any time of life. They can occur with no warning. What you need to do is tell yourself that you can handle the situation. It may well only be temporary, but the cause and effect may last for so much longer. However hard, or difficult, you can handle it. Stay calm, stay in control and take it slowly one moment, one step at a time. Do not let issues define you. Just be ready and aware of these moments when they occur. The more you know in advance, the more chance you will have of taking control, rather than sadly letting yourself become controlled.

Opportunities close both in front and behind you
With a sense of foreboding
Life can be duplicitous
You look for elucidation
You reflect seeking meaningful answers
You stay optimistic opportune
Relying on your astute aptitude
You stay gracious and grateful
The situation requiring perseverance
Maintaining a balanced, positive mental attitude
You use this period wisely
Perhaps even finding potential isolation necessary
Friendship is always utterly important
Manifestation helps you grow
A new chapter is awaiting
It is yours to write
So, write it and make it amazing.

We usually only think of a door as being just a door, which sadly means we miss the meaning of how they relate to new openings and ideas into different aspects of your life. If we continually hold on to the past, find that change is difficult, then we can never move forwards. Releasing and letting go, being always ready, is the only way to open those doors to your future. Allow yourself to let the past become the past, and not a torturous continuation of your life going forwards into the future. Look forward to the opportunities that await, which will appear in time. Let them happen, so that the adventure of your life will continually have other doors that open. Remembering when one door closes, another will be there, ready for opening elsewhere. Although it may not instantly become clear, those that close, close for a reason.

Remember to let issues go
Do not let those annoying problems linger
Those nagging harmful thoughts
They grow into more than situations
They become major problems
Which annoy and constantly drain
Forget about all of them
Why and what has happened
It happened in the past
Wipe it clean and start each day anew
A fresh, untouched slate
With a heart that is ready
Let your mind be clear
Forget about that which is gone
Let it be gone for good
Move on with obvious intention
Ready and receptive.

Always let your love and your kindness always show and shine. It costs nothing, so share it freely, widely and graciously. Not only will it make you feel good about yourself, but the help you give to those in need is unlimited and priceless. Every day is a new challenge, not just for you, but for so many others, too. So, whatever we can do to help will mean so much. You are doing great exactly as you are, just keep doing what you do. Your thoughts, your actions, signify who you are. They will not go unnoticed or unrewarded. Believe in yourself, you are amazing. You will never regret being kind. So be kind always, because you never know who is in need, or when you will need kindness reciprocated in return. What you give, you will always get back. Keeping balanced actions and thoughts.

A painting starts with a first brush stroke
A book starts with the first word
A journey begins with that first step
Everything starts with a thought
Ideas grew into plan and germinate
Those inner embers bursting into flame
They are all equally important
As is the connection between the start and the end
That first thought and then the ultimate moment
But what comes in between is down to you
Making it what you want
It is your life step by step
Deciding what to try to what to experience
Try something new or try again
Either way, just keep trying
If we never try, we will never know
By trying, you may just amaze yourself
So, make a start and find out more about you
Do not wait to be given ideas
You have your own; they are yours to use.

Time really does not stand still; it is never ceasing and moves forward relentlessly. Whatever you choose to do today, keeping doing it with complete faith, hope and love. Staying true to your own song, the one that sings deep inside, the one which resonates with your heart and your soul. You are the only one who knows what that song or tune is, so never worry about what others may think. They have their own. You know yours vibrates with you, and always will. You are full of the magnificence of the universe, your light, your love. It is there and will never run out, so use these freely with abundance. Make your time, here on Earth a time of rejoicing and joyfulness, supply your God given abundant gifts, freely, far, wide, and daily.

Happiness comes from the heart
You cannot go out and buy it
Neither can we can make it
There is no illusion
It does actually exist
To find it, use the magic
The magic which is you
This starts the process and makes it happen
Allow it to manifest and to grow
Let your magic flow fast and free
Today and always and forever
Your spirit lives within you
Let it always show you the way
The way to live and love your life
Do not just imagine that this can happen
Everything is possible
Even what we think is impossible
Live and enjoy
No one else can do it for you.

However strenuous life can be, we must endeavour to utilise the time we have, to use it to the best of our ability. Some days are easy, others are so much tougher than we may have predicted or expected. Take each new day, the best you can, and in your stride. Handle with aplomb, whatever comes your way, however stressful or difficult. It is so easy to waste and lose time, but once it is gone, it cannot come back. Although we may get a second chance, that may use up even more valuable time and effort another day. Every difficult moment makes us want to forget about the situation and to drift, which we then do without clear thought from one day to the next. Try to be always in charge of yourself, and not to let this happen. Keep a focus of intent, allow your thoughts to remain positively high, forget about what has gone, and accept any issues as being part of your daily test and continual growth. Storms do eventually blow themselves out.

I was feeling completely fogged
Totally clogged within
There was nothing coming
No flow of thought
Like an old rusty tap
Broken, unusable and defunct
However hard I tried
No movement, it was stuck tight
I took time out for me
I thought deeply, long and hard
There had to be a way
An idea slowly appeared
A solution formulated
What I was looking for was there
Deviate find a different source
Find an alternative route
There is always alternate way
Acceptance that options exist
With patience, you may find the answer
To set you back on your right path
Enabling you to move forward
Along a new direction, with positivity.

As we know, each day is different and a new opportunity to develop and experience life. Today cannot be the same as yesterday. They are never quite the same twice. Of course, we can feel a deep sense of connection and familiarity, because of most days being similar, giving us that continuing connection between past, present and future. So, ensure you make the most of who you are, and with the time that you are here. More than anything, love yourself and who you are. It is your life. We only get this opportunity once, so ensure you never waste it. Have a day full of positive thoughts and thankful gratitude. If you allow yourself to be stressed, then anguish will result. Accept what is and will be. Let your love always be your shining light. Make sure every moment is enjoyable. Time slips by so quickly and is gone, yes it has already disappeared whilst reading this.

What was?
What is?
What could be?
Are all parts of the same
Three interlinking elements
All unknown lessons of life
Lessons which happen as we learn along the way
If you allow the past to haunt you
It could so easily affect you in the present
Or even potentially ruin a better tomorrow
Remember to live in the here and enjoy the now
What has gone is over and finished
So, leave it there in the past
That which is still to come has not yet materialised
Acceptance is the key to finding your respective doors
Leaving behind those which are well and truly closed
Realising many doors still await unseen
They will hold many untold unknown secrets
In time, they will eventually reveal all
However hard we try, we cannot hasten it.

Like a never-ending spiral, the whirlpool of life can constantly pull us deeper and deeper inwards. If we cannot take care and sensible precaution, too easily are we drawn into a situation, and pulled downwards. The resulting action then becomes beyond our control. If this happens, you could become dragged inwards, and getting back out again then is more and more difficult. There is a point at which, where the chances of absolutely no return, becomes highly probable. We need to do our utmost to ensure that this event does not happen. If occasion should arise, where necessary, hold out and look for a helping hand. There will always be one readily available, but when needed, we need to have the strength and foresight to ask. Never ever be too proud to seek help, whatever the situation, sometimes you just cannot manage it all by yourself alone. Put pride and proudness to one side, before the inevitable occurs, and that maelstrom has you caught forever.

Turn problems into opportunities

Show yourself love and your kindness

Accept that life constantly changes and develops

When necessary, spend time somewhere quiet alone

Breathe, sit, relax and rest

Learn to focus on taking each step one at a time

Slow down to relieve the build-up of stress

Let go of unwanted, harmful emotions

Stop and take time out completely for you

Connect with the wonder which is nature

Let fresh air and exercise aid your health

Set regular temporary breaks each day

Release and let go of your worries

They serve no purpose other than more worry

Looking after yourself is important

The welfare of you and your body matters.

We have a forever flowing fountain inside. A fountain which is of the purest love and most abundant light. There is never any worry about it running dry. It has been there always and was with you from the day that you were born. It is continual, never needing topping up, a blessed gift that we all have. The more we give, the more we share, we more we can give, a sublime process of continual giving. So, allow this to happen and flow each day, constantly freely, day after day. The force and flow will develop and grow over time, becoming stronger, more intense, and beneficial. Your own connection, and your clarity of thought, will also increase. It is a completely universal solution where everyone gets rewarded. So be love, be light. Be your own connection to the divine, which is living within us all. All we need to do is believe. Believe in who we are. Never stop believing in you, keeping thinking I am love, I am light. You are so full of love and light and always will be. This is such a true blessing.

Make your life your own life
Always be yourself
You will play many roles
There will be struggles
It may never seem to be just plain sailing
You will occasionally need to make a stand
But be inspirational, open and willing
Leadership may not be a strength
But try to lead by example
Be an example of kindness, compassion, and love
Why hide yourself away?
The world needs you
Stay visible and approachable
Put yourself first
Never put yourself last
You are enough, just as you are
You are truly loved, and so lovable
Love yourself too
You are exactly where you need to be
In time we you will be somewhere else
But do not force changes
Let them occur, as they should
At their own pace and time.

Our thought processes can so easily make us think and feel like someone who is not us. The mind is so powerful and complex that it can so easily take over and rule us. We need to be constantly aware of this happening, which is done far too often. Unless we can prevent this, we will never, ever have full control over who we are. It is difficult to find the required focus, but unless we do, we find that our ensuing negative thoughts become more dominant. They take control of all situations and become the identifiable source of who we are. It is vitally important that you practise controlling your thought process, knowing where they come from, and how you respond to them. No one else can do this for you. Have control over your mind, not the other way around. Know who you are, not who you are not. Do not allow it to lead you into places from which you will find you have no control or means of escape. The mind is powerful, but you are more powerful, so use your resilience with astute awareness. Just be aware, and always pay attention to yourself!

There is always a light somewhere
We are never completely in the darkness
Even in an unilluminated night we sense a glimmer
We just need to keep believing
When in need, you may need to search yourself
Your light will always be there
It will never disappear and will forever be with you
Believe, have faith, have trust, and hope
Never think that it has abandoned you
Your soul has been within you always
It has never left you
It never will because it is your essence
Home is not where you live
That is a just house where you inhabit
It is that place within you
It has and always will be there
In your heart, your soul
The way home to you lies within
Never feel desolate or lost
You are the way home
When in need, it is easy to find
The answer and the way home to you.

As another day heads towards the close, it is that time when we delve deep within the mind and awaken our soul. What journey of wonder and adventures await tonight? Will we visit places we know well or go way beyond our wildest daytime thoughts or dreams? Until it happens, no one knows the answer, so trust and allow the journey to take you far and wide. An exploration or a mission to find answers to questions which you never even knew were potential questions. Sleep with a clear conscience, whilst maintaining an open mind. Find out about fulfilment. Trust the Universe, it will guide you without fail. Your dream interpretation, in trying to understand it afterwards, is yours and yours alone!

Do not be hard on yourself

You are just perfect as you are

Keep going forwards and learning to growing

Trying and thriving

Seeds take their time to sprout

Even oak trees start from a seed

They cannot show their glory for decades

Just be you exactly as you are

You are truly your own hero

You are much stronger than you will ever think

The past or the future can never equal the now

Be happy and live in the present

Today is your present

It is a time for joyous living

Not a time for delay or waiting

Live your life your way

No one else can do this for you

Do it for yourself.

Appreciation may only be a word, but what a word, it is truly meaningful. The resulting actions that go with it are so much more than just a simple word. Just imagine life without gratitude, without sincerity, no I do not expect that you can, and neither can I. What a poor, ungratefully sad world that would be. It should just happen naturally, automatically, with none needed to add to the thought process. Even the most basic thank you should be a feeling of truly deep-felt respect. Remember to show this all the time. It is sadly so easy for this to be missed, for it not to happen, and to become overlooked. So, be truly appreciative, for everything, not occasionally when it feels right, but continually each day. Give freely and accept willingly.

Turn problems into opportunities

Think and then act

Show your love and your kindness

Life is constantly changing

When necessary, spend time alone

Take a breather, sit, relax and unwind

Learn to focus and take each step one after another

Slow down to help to relieve any stressful build-up Let go of unneeded emotions

They can so easily define you

Take time out completely for you

Connect with yourself to aid your health

Set regular temporary breaks each day

Make them a little thank you to yourself

Release and let go of your worries

They serve no purpose other than more worry

Connect with your senses, see, smell, feel, hear, listen

Use them to help you and your body and your life.

Today is another opportunity to move forward with your plans, plans for each of us will understandably vary. There will naturally be difficulties, but there is no need to stress over what you cannot control. If things take an unexpected turn, then accept that is how it is. Stay calm, even though your mind may try to control and dictate what you should do. Allowing yourself to stay in and have control is important. Consider options logically. We all are different, so what is good for one may not be good for another. Listen to your body, only you know how you feel, and how to act. There is no point running yourself into the ground. Life is a journey, not a sprint, taking each day as a separate segment, and balancing your needs accordingly. It is your life, your journey to find what is right and balances for you.

Your heart and soul are your essence
Connected like rivers and streams
They flow together
Forming something far stronger
Let them always blend
And add a touch of care and kindness
They make you who you are
A loving, joyful human being
Let yourself live your way
A free flowing, forever powerful spirit
Forever growing wiser
Sharing your love
Do not worry about others
Just never stop being you
Be magnificent, marvellous magical
Within you is the heart and soul of spirit
The essence of something far greater
A force so unimaginable
Full of the purest love
There is nothing greater or important.

Today, the focus is on anger, which can explode at any moment and unexpectedly from one second to the next. The answer to prevent this is to stay calm in all situations, not to react or to become angry. As this really is not what your spiritual self wants to see happen. Taking you away from the peace-loving person you are. It wants tranquillity, quiet, and calmness of thought and action. You will border the realm of danger. It at once thinks how I should respond, should I fight, or should I just accept the situation. Whatever that situation is, it is easier to walk away with grace and dignity. This may seem like capitulation, but walking away shows strength, not a weakness of character. So, when in doubt, do absolutely nothing. Stand up, keep calm, say nothing and walk away, have no comment, or need to look back. Removing yourself will automatically defuse the situation. If you react, then further action must happen. This is only natural. The Law of Equal forces will have applied. One action requires an opposite and counter action. By walking away, this action completes it, rather than fuelling the need for any further action. Think on this and how you can use it to your benefit, even in the mildest of potential issues.

Life is about control

Controlling ourselves

Controlling our thoughts

Not allowing ourselves to be controlled

Live without expectation

Live with trust and acceptance

Forget what I want, and I must have

Replace simply with what will be, will be

If it is meant, it will find a way

Trust and have faith in the process

The process of where your journey is taking you

It is not about how long it may take

How we learn and develop is important

It will all happen in its own time

If it does not happen, move on and look elsewhere

You do not have the no need to be concerned

Worry only causes concern, and even more worry

Allow life to flow along your chosen path

You may never know exactly where you are going

Allow the wonderful mysteries of life to unfold.

Make sure you start each day off with a smile, and then think clearly and steer yourself forwards. Going in the right direction, with a positive mindset, is paramount. When doing so, remember that whilst on your way, there is always something good to take from every day. Just be aware, and not blinkered in your views. Be more open, look, notice and feel. Feel that you are alive, not just living, and always be ready for those signs of synchronicity. They are everywhere. The art is to notice them, and to remember what they were. As one door closes, another is there, ready and opening. It may not always appear so, but have belief, faith, and trust in not only the Universe, but fully in yourself. Make today not just okay, or good, but fantastic. Even on the darkest, dullest of days, always be full of your own amazing sunshine and light.

We are told what to do
What we read
What we hear
What we see
We also talk about that
Information is everywhere
A continual overload
It can so easily confuse
It is with us now non-stop
Some of which may resonate
But more likely and potentially it may not
Assess it, filter, then accept or reject
Reason it out always in your mind
Using your own common sense
Logical thought allowing yourself to assimilate
Any or all individual differing viewpoints
Try to make up your own mind
This may be easier than you think
But remember, it cannot always all be at face value.

Today, as every day, choose to let your love shine out, so put on your sunniest, warmest, most loving smile. It is there waiting and freely available, totally unlimited, so share it far and wide. Be love, show love, and allow yourself to both freely give and receive love in abundance. The more you give, the more you will get. We know the Universe needs balance. So, no matter whatever your day beholds, whatever your destination today, just take it one step at a time. Allow yourself to be the purest love and light. You have it all inside. It will take you in the right direction, and it will help so many others, too. So, whilst helping yourself, and let yourself help humanity. Which needs the greatest help whilst we all struggle forwards day to day. Help starts within the heart, not just for yourself, but for others, too.

Always be gracious, grateful, and giving
Positively purposeful and practical
Keeping your feet firmly on the ground
Never expect, just accept
But have faith, trust and belief
Allow energetically enthused elucidation
Do not settle for befuddlement of thought
Embrace nothing but the truth
Through adaptability of aspirations
Forge your voyage of discovery
Tread your path with careful steps
Open your eyes fully to what the World offers
Look to achieve your ambitions
But do not despair if they take longer than planned
Live each day with a sense of moral obligation
An obligation to yourself and the way you live
Make living your life as a credit to yourself
Be an example for others to see, feel, and sense
So that they may use you as an example.

This is, as you already know is the next day of your life. So many will have gone before, leave yesterday's worries behind. Be alive, be ready, relax, breathe, share your love, and enjoy. It is another step along your journey. At the outset of each day, where it will take you is mostly unknown. There will be times within most days when you may feel slightly lost and very much adrift. There will be even, sadly, occasions when you feel potentially in pieces. These times will test your resolve, but they will also enable you to develop. You will become stronger, wiser, and more knowledgeable. When you feel broken, take time to put all the pieces slowly but surely back together. Make them more resolute than what they ever were before. Those openings will have helped let light in and allowed your own light to flood out. Although the damage may always be there deep inside and out of sight, it will have helped shape and made you who you are, and you will be proud to say I am whole again.

Sometimes I do not want to sleep
I feel it is unnecessary
My brain becomes active
But my body shouts for rest
Which way should I choose?
We spend so much of our lives asleep
Time that just drifts by night after night
Endless hours days weeks months years
Where has that time really gone?
We cannot quantify it as life
Although it is part of our experience
We may only have a brief reflection of it
A potential third of our lives unaccountable
In this dimension, sleep and we need rest
If it was not for this, just try to imagine
How much more we could achieve
How much more we could do
But then it would not be the life which we know
It is part of the balance which we need daily
Yes, I know I need sleep, but do I want it
There is no obvious clear-cut answer
Like so much in life, we accept it.

We again move once more into another day, the next one in which we take part in the game of life. A game as hard as any game you will ever play. Is it really a game? That is for you to consider and judge. What is important is how we learn and develop. Win or lose, each day you will have experienced many lessons. Some new, but many days will feel like those gone before. It may be as if you are trying to knock a hole in a wall or putting together a bridge to climb over barriers. It is all part of who you are and how you overcome a specific situation. There is always a way you just need to be unrestricted in how you look at differing points of view and situations. Try considering options logically, and which are realistically thought out before making a final decision. Defer making that choice, to allow yourself more time to evaluate ideas. A simple change of thought process can so easily put a completely distinct emphasis on what you want. Staying grateful, humble, honest, and respectful. Try your hardest and endeavour to do your best, but do not work yourself into a situation of a potential breakdown, either mental or physical.

If you are ever in need help
Please do not hesitate
You can rely on me
If you need advice or just want to chat
You know I will listen
If you need a shoulder
You know I have two
If you need a friend, a genuine friend
You do not even have to ask
If you need me, you know I am ready
Please contact me freely
Even if there is nothing you need today
You know I will be there tomorrow
Or whenever you need to make that call
It is a given, and I will not let you down
I have been there in need of help
It is without a doubt a lonely place to be
I do not want you being there ever
Together, we can overcome anything.

I do so believe that it will happen only when it happens. It can be at any age, young or old. The Universe does not count time, like we count time, it watches our development. That is when it occurs. We are and always will be Children of the Universe, no matter how old or who we are. We each have an agenda mapped out for us individually, which we agreed to before birth. When we appear as that person, the person we were always destined to be, there is no turning back. You may wait for what feels like forever. For this occurrence to happen. I know that I have waited for most of my life. This is my view, right or wrong, but I stand by this until proved otherwise. Each of us develops differently, and with unique traits and abilities. Find yours and allow yourself to find out who you really are.

Standing erect and proud
Bobbing joyfully in the summer sun
Hundred's even thousands of them together
Like an army of giants ready to march
Keeping each other company
Growing upwards towards the sun
A field of nonspeaking majestic heads
Sunlight, air, and water, that is all they need
They are a natural wonder
Bright and beautiful to behold
A magical shimmering summer reflection
Sunflowers everywhere you look by the score
You can be like them
Stand tall, proud, and upright
In times of cloud, they put their heads together
They share their light with each other
We need to follow their natural example
In times of need, we must light up each other
It certainly is easy, we all can do it
Just remember that two heads are so often better than one.

Life is tough enough without making it extra hard on yourself. When you need time for yourself. Make sure you take time out and take good care of yourself. If others offer to help or to lend a helping hand, make sure you take up that offer. Of course, be gracious and thank them afterwards, then let them know you will be there for them whenever that occasion may occur. What you give you, you receive back, and what you receive, you need to give. To keep the Universal Law of Balance in check, it works both ways. It is there for a reason. Life needs to be in balance, otherwise one aspect of life is out of sync with the rest of it. It is a simple, logical process, which we can all adhere to easily. Allow your life to be balanced in each respect.

Although perhaps never easy
Try to put yourself first
Never think of yourself last
Which we all so easily do
You are enough
Just as you are
You are a magnificent person
Full of unconditional love
So love, who you are too
Currently, you are exactly where you need to be
In time to come, you will be somewhere else
Do not look to force changes
That may cause a backward step
Let those changes occur in their own time
As they will at the opportune moment
Keep believe in yourself
Accept that there is a greater plan for you
Have faith and trust in the process
Believe that it will be worth waiting for
Many chances will come your way
Some which are intended, but others will vanish
Be brave and be ready for that leap of faith
Becomes when it comes, and it will
It will take you well beyond the norm.

Hopefully, today will be exactly as you imagine. A day should be smooth, easy-going, and with no unnecessary areas or reasons for stress. There are, however, always events that occur beyond our control. We may have carefully planned and imagine all will go like clockwork. Unfortunately, even clocks do breakdown, unexpectedly and without reason or warning. Be ready for fine tuning and adjust is necessary. Like all storms, which can come out of the blue, they will eventually pass. Let what happens occur, and then let it go. It will have happened for a reason. Like friendship, which may appear temporarily for a season, that season may continue and stretch and last your lifetime, potentially even many lifetimes. All we can do is accept how life is and let what happens happen. Go with the flow of life. It flows constantly, in and out, and we must allow the balance of both good with the bad. Take it step by step, one day at a time. Embrace and let life flow within you, and from outward to within.

Inside, of all of us, is an old inner warrior
Not one who wants to fight
Those days make no sense, as no one wins
One who loves life, and has a longing for peace
Harmony comes from just being you
Prosperity being far greater than actual wealth
The outer world is full of discord and discontent
It leaves your soul, heart and mind out of balance
Look deep inside yourself to find rebalance
That warrior is you and needs tranquillity
Dampen any battles raging deep within
Your life needs you to accept more and to want less
Courage is more than just a feeling
Delve deep and you will find it
It is there and always has been
When in need, find yourself
Take time to just be still
Listen, what do you hear
You hear nothing but yourself
That is the essence of blissfulness
Of your own place of nirvana.

We all make mistakes, have an error of judgement, that is a normal and a natural part of life. They may not happen every day, and not always of anything particularly meaningful, or of real long-term importance. If we learn from them, then they have taught us a lesson, however large or small, the significance. What we learn will then hopefully guide us forwards, and they will have been worthwhile. If we let these issues define us, then sadly we have not learned, and may continue to make the same mistakes continually. They become an increasingly heavy burden within our lives. Lessons occur for a reason; they help make us who we are and are all part of our continuing journey. We will never stop learning and will never stop making mistakes. It is all part of human nature and our journey. No one is prefect. Perfection is impossible. Just allow the lessons of life to shape you, your behaviour and thought patterns, and continue to make you a better and more rounded individual.

Find time to reflect within yourself
Answers you look for are waiting
We are here to learn the lesson of life
More and more we learn and search
We experience more and more.
Eventually, our knowledge increases
The whys, and the wherefores become clearer
The more you will get to know who you are
Analyse the information which flows
Helping you to learn and grow
Just be open to potential differing viewpoints
Grasp the meaning of each point separately
Consider them individually
Then carefully balance and decide for yourself
Your decision is your decision
It may be right or wrong
We cannot all come to the same conclusion
A difference of opinions is inevitable
Like you, I have free will
We make our own choices and decision.

We all need to think of ourselves as being like trees, strong and resolute. Sharing the differing seasons. Sometimes they help us grow and blossom. At other times, we slowly fade, hiding our beauty. Different times of year will appeal to us all. We always need to keep a constant and adequate supply of food, water and sustenance available. This is vital for our continued growth and wellbeing. Ensuring that both our outer and inner selves remain nourished, refreshed and cared for. In times of uncertainty, we need to let things go, just like the trees that shed their leaves each autumn. They have served their purpose and will no longer be of further importance. One element that stays constant is our ability to remain grounded and to keep our roots deeply connected.

The moon was full and as bright as day
Apart from a few light and wispy clouds,
The light shone in through the curtains
The sound of a splash awoke suddenly me
Looking out into the indigo blue darkness
I saw the brilliance of the moon's glare on the water
I could see what looked like ripples on the calm water
It may have been the tide or just the wind
It was hard to tell, but I would swear I could see something near the rocks
Did I spot the tail of a playful mermaid?
No, that was impossible
More likely my mind is half-awake playing tricks
A dolphin, even possibly a porpoise
More likely I thought
I looked and looked, but now nowhere to be seen
Whatever had been there was now out of sight
Back down in the darkness and depth
I will always believe but will never truly know
A touch of what the eye does not really see
Very much like life itself
A real conundrum.
I am just a piece of that puzzle
As you are all too.

Whatever today may bring, and every day is different, life can often just seem to be such a rush. The constant need to be here, then the need to get somewhere else in a hurry. It does not always have to be that way all the time. When necessary, allow yourself time, time to rest, recuperate, recover from the constant stresses that day-to-day life can bring. Slow down. Make sure you listen to yourself. Only you know how you feel. Even taking a short break period will help. It cannot always be all systems go; everything occasionally needs maintenance and servicing. We are no different, needing to take care and look after ourselves. Make sure you do that. Remember, you are as equally IMPORTANT as everybody else, because if you do not do this, no one else can do this for you.

What you desire is coming
Divine timing will not let you down
We cannot control it
It is waiting and will happen
But only when it happens
Patience is the focus and key
Allowing your thoughts to manifest
For those ideas to take shape
Allowing and accepting is important
We have so many thoughts each day
Make sure that they are on what you want
Not on those that you do not
Stay aware if they drift
Bring yourself back to the present
Always keep a positive mental attitude
Never become down beat
Believe in yourself and in your dreams.

The days come and go, they can just seem to roll one into another, and life can get even more mixed up than usual. Sometimes, we lose track of the day, and very often the date. During these periods, we need to ensure that we stay focused. Try keeping your feet firmly on the ground, staying in control of both yourself and your situation. As and when you can, get out into the sunlight, let those rays of goodness reach down deep inside, spreading the benefit which they bring. Spread your arms open wide, just sense and feel the wonder of nature. Try to imagine the size of the world in your hands, and the universe way beyond. Yes, it is far greater, more enormous than that sensed within our imagination. Let the wonders, which are freely there, reignite, refocus you, it is so easy to do. So, do it as regularly as you need. Your body, your mind, your life will be grateful that you did.

We all need to free ourselves from unwanted cords
Old attachments where there is nothing visible to see clearly, and
sweep them away
Allow them to disappear completely
Sent off into the vastness of time and space
Back to where they once came
Returning to whoever they once belonged
Freeing yourself from those unrequired bindings
Removing issues that tied you to your past
Even those of a far distant past lifetime
They are now of no importance no significance
All they do is cause uncertainty, doubt, and torment
They bring constant issues to your life
Visualise them attached to you
Then see them come cleanly away from you
Moving away into the depth and darkness
Only you can free yourself
So, set yourself free from those restrictive chains.

Do you always see things clearly? Can your judgement occasionally consider being out of place? It is so easy to judge without understanding or knowing all the facts. When we judge another, we break them down; we put them into compartments and separate them into different boxes. What we are, in fact, doing is comparing them against ourselves. Judging is easy, while understanding means we must look at things differently and from their perspective as well. We need to change places, see the situation from their angle in order not to judge at face value. Knowing what the overall and whole complete situation is matters. This allows for careful consideration, rather than judgemental single-mindedness. Do not just rush in making an instantaneous conclusion, take time to judge, to weigh things up, and find a balanced, quantifiable helpful long-term solution.

Do you ever have a sense of foreboding?
A feeling that something important will occur
Dead ends vulnerability, even isolation
A sensation of acrimonious abstinence
That realisation of potential impermanence
Having reached a crossroads of your creativity
One avenue slowly closing, coming towards the end
Requiring a refreshingly new coordinated concept
Keeping your feet necessarily firmly on the ground
Having a positively prosperous mental attitude
Not becoming frustrated, befuddled or delusional
Being decisively direct determined
Pathways await and doors will eventually open
Adaptability will enable accomplished achievements
Staying always true to yourself and your own values
Believing that, however tough a current situation
That potentially a better opportunity will occur tomorrow.

Taking time out to experience periods of reflective quiet and silence will always help you focus. To think on any issues, and to see if answers are there waiting. They will become clearer, so the more you practise this regularly, the easier it becomes to connect. It will give you the opportunity to find out more about yourself than you may already know, or even previously realised. There is no need to shut yourself away. Just take time regularly to sit and reflect peacefully. Meditation has so many benefits, and frequent practice well help to deepen the experience. It is so beneficial, in so many ways. You can practise this anywhere, including outdoors, where you can connect to the earth and fully ground yourself. Allow yourself this opportunity, because no one else can do it for you. So, make time to do this for yourself.

The clock keeps ticking

It never stops

Relentlessly forward

Second by second

Minute by minute

Hour by hour

Unseen, sensed, or felt

We just know that it happens

A concept way beyond our reach

Totally beyond our control

But so easily do we waste it

A precious commodity needing to be valued

It flows by and is gone instantly

Once gone, it is out of reach

You cannot get it back

So, use it, do not lose it

Control it, do not become controlled by it

Life and destiny both measured by time

Think of it as a precious commodity

Which you cannot store, and losing it is unaffordable

Time is the substance and the essence of life.

It is so important to have a collection of close family, and good fiends within your life. This does not need to be overly extensive, just people to be there for not just occasionally, but when urgent needs arise. When they most need help, and it becomes so important. Being able to listen, offer advice, considered guidance, direction, but kindness and support. Look after, care for, and protect them. They are more than just family and friends. Let the connections grow over time to become something unique. An amazingly strong bond, which will be inseparable and vital when you also struggle and need to reach out for their help. Never be too proud or stubborn when that need arises. The last thing you need is to feel like a remote island, isolated all alone, and without help at hand.

Pathways are there and take us along different routes
Different routes during the many stages of our life
At relevant times of our development
They appear as and when they needed
But may only take us part way towards our destination
The exploration enables us to develop
Journeys can be short, long, and involved
Each is a new or re-enforcing learning opportunity
Sometimes we get shown where we need extra help
Experience enabling us to understand
Each path will occur for a specific reason
Allow yourself to be brave and fearless
Live and love your adventures
Follow your dreams whilst you grow
It is your story, so make it enjoyable
Live each day with a gracious heart
Make the journey of your lifetime memorable.

Remember to keep your thoughts positively high and flowing. Favourable outcomes will follow in time. Let your mind make valued decisions, not rash choices. Balance and weigh options up, you will be thankful for taking this route. Show that you have a sound and balanced strength of character. Walk tall and with pride in each step. Show the world that you are confident, amazing, and ready not just for today, but every day. Avoid being pushed, pulled, or dragged downwards. Becoming discouraged can so easily occur. You are far better, stronger, and more deserving of encouragement and kindness than that.

Take yourself forwards with aplomb. Be grateful, show thanks and gratitude. Be proud of who you are, the journey you have taken, and what you have had to contend with getting to where you are. It has made it who you are. Never forget that ever.

I am the Universe and all planets within
Including everything else seen in your sky
The earth you feel under your feet
The mountains before your eyes
All the elements, including rocks and sand
Deep-rooted trees and plants
The smell of the flowers
Birds, bees and insects
All water, creatures and fish
The water you drink
The air you breathe
I am the sun giving light
The wind, rivers, seas, lakes and oceans are what I am
I am all elements of life
An unequalled force
Strong but benevolent and giving
All I am is within you too
I am the All, The Source, The Divine.

Start today off with giving kindness to yourself, then giving kindness to everyone else will just flow with ease. Let this be part of your daily morning routine. It will, in time, become second nature. You should also always celebrate yourself, each day, something that every one of us can do. So, start this process today, tell yourself how proud you are of your achievements, and, well, you have coped with adversity. Do this often and as regularly as you need. Be proud of who you are. Show yourself love, care, hope, and light, and show this freely to everyone else. Be the best version of yourself that you can be, enjoy your life and the joy which it brings, and be proud of what you have achieved. Just get through each day is an amazing achievement, and you should be proud of this at the end of each day.

We all experience the same
Choices good or bad
In the end, we do the best we can
Remember, the past has gone before
Day before night each day is different
Tomorrow we start again
It is not a virtual game; it is life
Our life, the only one we get
So please only think ahead
Do not reflect continually on that which has passed
The future is there, ready to knock at the door
Always answer with a positive yes
Be ready for opportunity when it shows
It will lead you forward onto greater times
Life is and what will be
So, make it the life you desire
Each day a new challenge
That is the wonder of life
Be prepared and expect
Ready to make the unexpected
To become the expected.

Befuddlement, uncertainty, self-deceiving, disconcertment, dead ends, doors closing, these can all be such totally confusing aspects, situations, even conundrums. Life is truly a mixture; we need to add the right ingredients to get our own required results. We ask where to next. This is constantly a question which there may not be an immediate or easy answer. Keep your motivation and spirits high, combine regular periods of meditative manifestation with your own individuality and integrity. Be energetic and open yourself in readiness for the journey which lies ahead. You are the key to the solution. Unlock yourself and open the doors which are there waiting for you. You are the only one who can do this, think clearly, be brave, and experience those forthcoming encounters with a readiness of spirit within.

Solutions and problems
They come circling around
Your find thoughts and suggestions
Are they solutions or just potential problems?
Which way should you turn?
That is never the easiest of decisions
To look for the correct answer
The problem may have many options
But choosing the correct solution is never easy
And does the solution solve the problems?
It may just cause even more which were unseen
Whichever way you look or decide
It will not be straight forward
Although looking ahead is the only correct option
Do not allow yourself to force that which is looked for
The result may, in time, enable you to find an answer
Does this help or really resolve the equation?
More spiralling thoughts will swirl through the mind
They fly around filling up, confusing your thoughts
Whichever way you look, indecision is always close
You will eventually need to decide what is for the best
Potentially just taking a chance to find a solution
It is never a clear-cut situation
In the end, you can only do what you feel is best
Time will give an answer to the rest.

We all grow and develop differently, and at the speed intended for us. Sadly, it is all too easy to presume, and then march forwards blindly without real purpose or a logical plan. Forever, going onwards and expecting everybody to step out of our way. Even to the point of potentially rolling over submissively. Would that possibility make life easier than it is? I fear not, as blindfolded judgemental vision is so easy, but just is not the answer. It is full of negative action, rather than positive focus and thought. Weighing up all the reasons, the situations, considering the other person's views and perspective, are vital points of the process. Before supplying help, we will have a far clearer picture of their situation. So before making irrational and illogical judgement, take time to listen and to consider. Understand their alternative position. Learn to accept that we may not be correct in our assumptions. Acceptance always helps. Continually to grow, to find a way, because there is always one to find.

When you're feeling down, nothing else seems to matter
Thoughts play upon the mind like leaves buffeting in the wind
You try to find answers for which there seems no reason
You constantly question and search for a solution
Thoughts go round and round in an ever-increasing spiral
Constant longing to resolve the situation
Continually stuck, unable to find your path
Feeling lost in the darkest forest
Will you ever get to know why
Will it just be a case of having to let go?
That question itself is a conundrum
Which potentially has not an easily answer
All you can do is to manage and get through
Eventually, it will become the past
You manage life in the present
Knowing you will eventually move forwards
In the meantime, you will always wonder why and what was this all about.

Each day comes and is gone. Some feel far too quickly. They sense the need for more time every day. So, the sooner plans and ideas are in place, the better it will be. Over time, we will all have made mistakes by not being ready. This is quite natural. Accept them for what they are, learn the intended lesson, and then forget about them. Consider how they coped in days gone by. Their situations were without a doubt trial and error, practised repeatedly. They learned and prevailed, without the advantages of the technology which we have at our fingertips. So, be humble, think of the courage and fortitude they had, then manage any necessary process and find a new way. Forget about that I cannot do this mentality, and it is beyond me. Look at options with an open mind and find that alternative route. Amaze yourself, and then reflect and say yes, I did it and be proud of the achievement.

Today will differ from yesterday
Some days will naturally be easier
Others so much more difficult
It is a case of taking the good with bad
The rough with the smooth
The easy with the tough
Juggling becomes part of your daily act
Trying to keep everything constantly moving
Staying mentally physically emotionally strong
Overcoming issues, obstacles, and setbacks
Allowing yourself to stay focused with determination
Doing your best and constantly trying
Managing all situations and prevailing time after time
Moving forwards and not dwelling on past events
Living in the here and now
Managing your life with balance
Accepting that the outcome may not be desirable
Understanding that it will have occurred for a reason.

Belief is a unique consideration, and of the utmost importance, and how we all look at things differently. A painting, the clouds, and, of course, life will never appear the same for two. Similar thoughts and views, yes, that much may well naturally occur, but they will not be entirely the same. Life is very much like this, too. What appeals to one will not appeal to another. We cannot be equal, because we are not the same. We are all individuals and have the choice of free will within this life. Understanding another person's point of view and their choices is so important in accepting how the balance of life works. The understanding behind the concept which we have within the life which we experience. Do not take a dogmatic view, be pragmatic with your thoughts, your comments, and actions.

Do you believe in consequences?

They are pivotal for so much in life

If I had not done this or that

Then what occurred could not have happened

They had not invited, I could not have gone

The thought may not have started, becoming an idea

A chain of random but interlinking events

Everything being connected by actions

Primarily by our thoughts, resulting in actions

Each action results from a process

Which does not just happen by chance

Neither does chance, just occur either

It is never an incidental accident

Accidents result from an action

Each thought is an action of a consequence

Although each thought is not necessarily directly connected

The connection between them occurs because of actions

Thought processes lead the way to the formulation of an action

Actions being a major part of how mindfulness works

Working with you to create more actions

Have faith and belief in them as they are

They are never accidental

We mean each purposefully

These actions continue your ongoing life process.

If we need to change things, firstly look and change yourself. Look at all situations, wonder and say I am not limiting myself by my actions and or my beliefs. The worst thing you can do is to put an actual label on yourself. Why would you consider doing this? There is no need to worry about being pigeonholed. Just say, I will not be stuck again as I was. I am free to fly. I will not be subject to restrictions or held back by any set of parameters. If you have no way to fly, you are self-imprisoned, with no way of escape. Just simply be who you are. Allow yourself to root deeper, grow stronger, expand, develop, and grow. Allow the Universe to worry about who you are eventually going to be. It was all planned and predetermined before birth. You must just follow along the route map of your life, and the journey which sends you onwards daily. This will eventually bring you far greater happiness and clarity. Expect nothing to happen, just accept that which does. I know plans may not always seem logical, but sadly, that is part of the essence of life. Illogical logic allows each of us to be the individuals which we are.

We all need to trust

To trust in ourselves and in the wait

Taking nothing for granted

Because nothing is ever certain

Believe though in yourself

Have faith in who you are

Trust in loyal friends

They are rare, like precious jewels

Your life is yours to live

Experience and enjoy your adventures

Just like an old-fashioned lucky dip

You never knowingly are sure one day to the next

Take what comes your way with a smile

We never know exactly what lies ahead

Your dreams, your desires will change as you change

All moving slowly forwards

Eventually they may just come to hand

Nothing is completely certain

If it was, then life would not be the life we know.

Which is more important the participation, or than the actual result? If we don't take part, then we will never know. We will never learn, develop, or find new or necessary life skills. We all naturally, of course, want to succeed, and to feel like winners. But not to win at all costs, that is not the solution. Life is very much the same. How we handle it makes such a difference. It is a like game, a game of chance. There are many risk factors built in. Unless we try, take that step, there is no way we will ever know. We might succeed, we might fail, but we will have found something out about ourselves that we did not know before. They both teach us lessons, lessons of our life. From this, we either continually fail, rethink, or change our direction. Considering unfamiliar processes can move us forward, even helping us to win. If we never do it for ourselves, however much external encouragement we receive, it will not happen. Nothing ever comes of nothing. Whatever your endeavour, stick with it as it will eventually bring results. Keeping trying until those results are acceptable and meet with your expectations.

I am imperfectly perfect or perfectly imperfect
Is there really any accurate definition between either
That is a question for others to judge and decide
Although that is, of course, difficult, as they will also be one or the other
So, all we can do is accept that which is as what it is
Why do we need to judge others, anyway?
What right do we have to consider whether we are superior or they are inferior?
We should all consider each other as equals who have differing skills sets
The hierarchical structure currently used will always place one above another
This will put multi-layers of subordinates underneath
Which will have both advantages and disadvantages
But in life we need to consider all as equals
Irrespective of any imperfections
Remember, you are who you are with imperfections
But you have potential and many perfect qualities
Value the friendship of your friends
They are who they are, and exactly as they should be
Thank them all for being who they are.

Everything happens, happens for a specific reason. Sometimes, sadly, it all goes wrong, for reasons well beyond our control. We cannot understand why it has occurred, or for what has been the cause. We may never know completely why. Certain things occur just to refocus us, and to realign us along our chosen spiritual life path. All we can do is accept that which occurs, is for the best, and try to understand the hidden wherefores and the whys. Good times, bad times, indifferent times, even unexpected situations, they all happen all the time. They test our resolve, and constantly do so over, and over, and over again. No one ever said that life was going to be easy. Why should it be easy? What would we learn to take forward if this was the case? Most of the answers which we look for may just remain as unresolved questions, or in time only provoke more unanswerable questions. We must just accept what is, leave that which will be, and understand that occurrences happen. Life is more complex than we could ever fully imagine or completely understand. It is constantly flowing, on the move, and always only ever more in a forward direction.

Our thoughts can hold us captive
Prisoners of the mind
Free yourself from this
Let yourself be free
You can do this with belief
Have faith, trust and just believe in you
Allow your light to bring happiness
Not just to yourself, but to others too
Overcome daily obstacles as they occur
Remove negativity and deep-rooted doubt
Prevent those nagging, niggling buds from taking hold
They will easily grab you and prevent your thought process
You will, with practise, be able to resist this at will
Freeing your mind and allowing yourself complete control
If you can do this, and you can
You can have control over your life
Rather than life having control over you.

Some of us can survive so much more easily than others. Is it always survival of the fittest? No, I believe that is not necessarily the case. Pain is felt, suffered, endured differently, and in so many ways for each of us. Physical, mental, emotional, and even spiritual pain are all connected, but different. They become grouped as a generalisation together. When we hear of someone in pain, we automatically think of it being physical and something noticeable. But sadly, this is not the case, as much is out of sight, and behind the curtains of life, deeply hidden within the mind. Although not always easy, try to ensure that others are never allowed the opportunity to control your mind, and also your life. Never let their actions affect yours. What they choose to do is their choice, not yours. Stay within the calmness that you have, show that your strength runs deep within, and your intelligence can overcome your emotions. If issues become serious and become too great to handle by yourself, put pride to one side, seek help, care, support firstly from friends, and if necessary, trained professionals.

Believe in yourself, your future, and your dreams
Relax and breathe deeply
You enough as you are and always will be
Who we have with us in our lives matters
Material things are far less import
Setting and getting our priorities right
Friendship happiness honesty, that loyal bond
Being there during the good times is great
But being there in the tough times is even more important
Sharing emotions laughing smiling and even crying consoling together
Life is an and always will be a rollercoaster ride
Constantly up, and then down
Hardly ever smooth and never stopping
Take each day of your journey on its merits
Never expecting, just accepting that which will be
Live each day separately because that is what they are
Although they get linked and looked at as a whole.

An easy start does not guarantee long-term success. Whereas taking time to learn, to plan, gives every possibility of sustainable viability. We see this everywhere, and within every aspect of life. Development is the key. It enables thoughtful progress, and a carefully focused, considered approach. Patterns become established, resulting in good practices, whatever and wherever the need may be for in life. Use this analogy wisely and to your advantage. Do not just jump in at the deep end. Take your time. There is never the need to rush, and then find yourself almost at once struggling, way out of your depth and your comfort zone. Plan carefully, take each action slowly, methodically and step by step. Then execute those thoughts intelligently, astutely, and with dynamic precision. Giving yourself a balanced and beneficial opportunity, in the long-term, to succeed, rather than failing before your venture has even started.

Do you ever feel life has trapped you?
The constant ebbing and flowing
Being as if you are floundering between two seas
Or coming in with the fast-flowing tide
Then retreating again as the cycle alternates
Waiting patiently for the schedule to reoccur
Just like the sequence between earth and moon
Life constantly goes around regularly
Everything continually revolving
The earth, the planets and all the solar system
We are all connected and all part of the same universe
There is a fixed timetable and set elemental pattern
Will we ever fathom it completely?
Or find the magic formula
To solve one of life's many conundrums
Allowing life to become clearer
To enable us to learn more about ourselves
It is impossible to say if we will
All we can do is take each day, one at a time
Accept what will be, will be and let it occur
Allow the flow of life to take you on our journey.

Today, like every other day, is going to be a day of stepping forwards, onwards, but not backwards. Another day within the mystery and the riddle of life, which it undoubtedly is. Life is a paradox, full of constant puzzles, some of which will not be easy to solve. They can even nearly take forever to find the relevant answer, and some potentially never. Constantly inundated, coming from all sides with daily triggers; we may not think of them that way, but they are. It is how we handle them that matters. If we are reactive or proactive to these situations. There can be such a fine line sometimes between the two, even the smallest incidence can cause the biggest of reactions. Provocation is constant, and from all sides. Being aware that it can happen at any moment makes such a difference. It will mentally prepare you in case of any, and all, eventualities. You are ready to take control, to take them these issues in your stride. Ready to defuse situations before they boil over, exploding into major out-of-control confrontation. We are and have the answer to so many situations and their solutions. Staying prepared, ready to expect events before they occur, is vital.

Do you ever feel you are being sucked towards a black hole?

To somewhere unknown and inescapable far away

Your thoughts can often happen and feel this way

Life can seem as if you are being dragged towards potential oblivion

Just as something has pulled you into a million separate pieces

To have that disjointed discombobulated sense of bewilderment

Wondering why this happened and where are all your missing parts

Your thoughts are all over the place and nothing making logical sense

Slowly but surely, you need to edge yourself back together

To find the wholeness, that is you once more

It is natural to go through all these stages of evolvement

They are part of the journey of your life, your development

When you reappear afterwards, you are stronger

A more aware version of the person than you were before.

Inspiration, inspirational, motivation, motivational, simply when or where, will you find encouragement through actions, words, and deeds? We constantly need to stay motivated, and to find inspiration. This can either be by inspiring yourself or being the example to others and aiding them in the best way possible. By pushing ourselves, we can take a different path within our life journey, which may lead us to amazing discoveries. We are all pushed each day, mostly to our limits, and all we can do is try our hardest to do our very best. Life is about give and take. Staying mentally and physically strong is vital. It is not about who is the toughest; it is about being the smartest and using your knowledge and abilities wisely. So, use your imagination occasionally, let it run wild. By starting this process, it will amaze you how creative you can be. Use it for your benefit, and for that of others. Being a help and helping brings rewards both ways.

We are part of a circle within a circle
There is no start
It is timeless
Continual progression
What has been before
Will return and come around again
The journey having begun long ago
Our ancestors and their forebears were part
All rooted deep inside the continual journey
The sun, the moon, they have seen it so many times
We are all of our planet, and of the earth
Connected to everything here and the stars beyond
We need to show and provide continual for ourselves Plus as much
love for the planet
It is our foreseeable forever home
It needs protecting and preserving
Look after it well, let it support and provide for you
Without this, we will eventually lose it
Lost within the Universe and without a home.

Constantly changing, and nothing ever standing still. How life has always been, and always will. Everything is always on the move and in permanent motion. We need to believe the plan the Universe has, even if we cannot see it. It will guide us forward accordingly. We may not know which course it will take us, but like the Phoenix, who rises from its ashes, we must always rise from the ashes of our past. We can then look forward, when needed, knowing that what is gone is gone, and what is due is a brand-new and hopefully better opportunity. Never be afraid of rebirth. It may be just what you have been waiting for all your life. Walk through the process and start the cycle again. You may need to do this many times before you find your true path. The only one making this specific journey is you, so trust and believe in yourself. Have faith in every step you take. You are on a constant journey of discovery, constantly finding out about yourself. Never think, never only think of opportunity, potential, and new beginnings.

I do so believe that what I mean will be
Always be ready for the unexpected
What lies ahead is for now unknown
Keep a positive and open mind
Opportunities will occur out of the blue
They may send you off in a new direction
A direction taking you forwards
There is always a starting point
So, be ready for that moment
Because it will just happen
Commencement of a fresh experience
Part of the ever-unfolding adventure of life
When they happen, take the opportunity
It may never reoccur and come again
The Universe doesn't count time
It watches our development
No matter how old, age is irrelevant
Each of us develops differently
We are all children of the Universe
Our paths are all different
We cannot rush them
They will strengthen overtime.

Another day, and another opportunity to focus on growth, where you want to be and how you are going to get there. Each day allows you to move a little closer towards the life goals, along your path. Even tiny steps forward will be an improvement in where you were before. Never have regrets. Some days are easier and more memorable than others. Every day is full of adventure, wonder, and excitement. Something simply known collectively it as LIFE. Life is a quest and about trying to be the best you can, even when things are not going quite to plan. Think of each day as a door, a door you have never seen before or tried to open. You do not know what is there behind it. There will be many possibilities, learn to accept what occurs and to never expect. That way, you will not be disappointed, and you will be more than likely pleased with what happens. Stay focused, positive and ready.

Life is never just right or just wrong
It is far more involved
More complicated and complex
An ever-changing daily itinerary
Each day having a different course structure
Acceptance is paramount
Change will always occur
But when you make time for yourself
You make time for your life
When you do not make that time
Your life is like an endless prison sentence
Never let yourself live behind invisible bars forever
Bars that limit you being the real you
The only person who can prevent this is you
Find time to find out about yourself
Take time-out and retreat
Free yourself from those parameters that restrict
Open your mind to exploration and knowledge.

Mental baggage constantly carried with you from the past is within you always, and unseen by others. We have these overbearing burdens with us each day. Obstacles which are still dragging on energy levels. Pulling us in all directions, other than the one we seek. A constant depletion of both thought and motivation. Will lead to a lack of enthusiasm and effort. So difficult to shake ourselves free, however hard we try. Readiness to start the process is paramount. Taking that first positive step forwards is the hardest but most vital. With full concentration of mind and concerted effort, it is achievable! Your inner strength enables determined focus. Gather your thoughts and plan a productive process. That ladder is ready and waiting for you. Do not wait. Take it rung by rung upwards and onwards.

Is it within your mind or mine?
Living there within you
Your own direct connection
Source being instrumental in your life
Your abeyance of thought
Energetic passive contact
Inward and outward channels directly open
Allowing different areas of insight
Deeping patterns of knowledge
Limitless journeys of exploration
You are but a soul within a vessel
Experiencing life and creation
Enjoying the opportunities that occur
Here for a time in human form
But continually moving and floating
Forever onwards within your journey
Through universal time and space
Use the connection you have
Open your awareness and yourself.

Life is very much about equilibrium, getting everything within it into harmony, and into place. If one element is out of step, then the whole situation suddenly becomes precarious, and potentially as if you're standing on a precipice. Looking down may just bring angst, and a feeling of deep-rooted uncertainty and trepidation. When it is all balanced, as it should be, life will be full of happiness, gratitude, and blissful. Sadly, this is often not the case. All we can do is what we can do. We have relatively limited time to do all that we may want. Survival is something which we rarely consider, but in the end we all need to look to survive. It is not a game where we get unlimited tries. It is our own real life which may sometimes seem like a dream, even a bad dream which you cannot get out of however hard you try. Life has no simple choices; we are here for whatever reason and scenario we have chosen. Enjoy it, love it, loath it, it is the one we picked. It is a test, a test of us and how we can cope with living as a human species.

Perfectly possible
Imperfectly impossible
Perfectly impossible
Imperfectly possible
Where does it start?
Where does it end?
One against the other?
No set rationale
No real reasoning
Judgement of the mix
What we get is our life
Each different, but thrown together
Never the same
We are not the same
Although we are similar
Actions and thoughts
Help figure out who we are
Living a perfectly imperfect
Possibly, impossible life.

You again have another opportunity to write a new chapter within your story. The story which is your life. A life which is constantly unfolding. Hopefully, today it will be a chapter which you will want to keep. You will never quite know what to expect, so always be ready to expect the unexpected. Hopefully, it will include a fair share of enjoyment and happiness. Which naturally makes any day so much easier than those which feel as if you are living under a dark cloud. We all get to experience both aspects of life within our chapters, those days which we love, and sadly those that we would just happily rather forget. The balance between the two enables a broader experience of the life we live. They help to shape our development, and all we can do is accept them on their individual merits. So, whatever today may bring, the ups, the downs, the smiles even frowns, just realise and let the flow happen. What is and will be within your journey will always occur as intended. Irrespective of our plans, it will ultimately happen.

Always believe that there is a plan
A plan in place for you
It may not be visible
But it is there waiting for you
Waiting like a shadow
There as a part of you
As and when it happens
It will be revealed and unravelled
Divine timing has its own schedule
It does not work within our own beliefs
Time is an elusive concept of our own making
It controls us way more than we think
Imagining beyond this notion is difficult
It is ingrained deep within
Stay focused on and with staunch belief
That which is coming will arrive in time
When all is in place and ready
It will then amaze you
Until that moment
Just take every opportunity you can to develop.

It is a new day, and a new opportunity to be you and to shine. Encourage, inspire, but do not stress if unexpected issues arrive. Instead, smile, laugh, be happy, and be that friend who does not hesitate to lend both hands. Start each day as a new opportunity, focus on building for your future, and where in time you want to be. Looking forwards is far more important than looking back where you have been. We cannot change the past but can plan and endeavour to make the future a far better story. So, why use up energy and thought processes on what has gone and where you have been? This is a waste of not only valuable time, but your energy. Look forward to where you are going. We are always moving in that direction, backwards where you have already been, is now in the past, your past and we cannot turn the clock back.

Acts of selfless kindness
Is there anything more generous?
Why when how they occur
It never really matters
Spontaneous deeply heartfelt actions
They naturally happen unexpectedly
No pre-planning or prior forethought
Just pure spur of the moment
But they are timely and needed
Allow them to happen
Give them frequently
Receive them willingly
They are magical moments of life
Tiny little amazing miracles
Full of unconditional love
Give kindness always
Not only you will feel better
The shared experience will benefit the recipient
It is most definitely an all-round winning situation.

Irrespective of whatever plans you may have today, just remember, kindness costs nothing. Allow yourself to be happy. Frequently and sadly, you will pick up negative energies from sources. They drag you down, draining and leaving you feeling lost. Like being lost, and all at sea within yourself. When necessary, ask the Universe for protection to be put around you, to help prevent this from occurring. Allow yourself a period of quiet, take time for thoughtful reflection, and connect and speak with your guides, guardians, and angels. Focus on your thoughts. Allow your own guiding internal compass to bring you back into natural alignment with yourself. Do this as often as you need. It is essential that you do this to remain positively balanced.

There is only one of me
There is only one of you
Only one of all of us
We are all individual and unique
With amazing abilities and talents
Never become compromised
Do not allow yourself to be suppressed
Stay true to how you are, and to yourself
Live your life, your way
It is your life to live
Enjoy your time as a human being
It is a relatively fleeting experience
Your journey is what it is
It is a test, your test
Let yourself flow each day
Do not take life too seriously
Learn to enjoy it
Love the experience
Try not to waste it
Make each day count
It will sadly be gone all too soon.

Today may already feel like a good day! Like a day with that feeling of energetic sunshine, warmth and light. An ideal opportunity to get outside and enjoy what the World can offer for free. There is so much, and sadly, we take it all for granted. So, rather than sitting back and thinking, take time to explore, to feel the wonder and the amazement of life. Use and utilise time to your advantage. So easily do we let it slip away, and through our fingers unnoticed. All problems will eventually fade away. It may take time, but they will never last forever. If you let them linger, you deny yourself the opportunity to move forward. Although they may temporarily hold you back where you are, and for a while from where you are going, given time, just like the seasons, they will change. The answer to everything is to have patience. However much we want to rush situations, sometimes it is just not possible.

Is being judgemental an excess of judging?
Usually happening without knowing the full facts
It brings about issues which become complex problems
Why would we want to be doing this?
Is this purely unknowing or just resentment?
Being envious truly is the next step
Seeing that others have so much more than you
Why should that be an issue?
We all are here to undertake our own journey
A journey of learning and of discovery
To find out why you are here and about yourself
You do not need to worry about others
Let them worry about themselves
Put yourself foremost
Be concerned about who you are
Your potential lack of knowing
Ask why does this issue matter?
Petty greed is like a virus
It becomes an ingrained illness
It takes over your feelings
Your actions become irrational illogical
Do not judge without all the facts
A presumptive assumption has no grounds.

People come and go in our lives. Some enter for a specific reason; others just appear for perhaps a season. What happens we may think that it is all within our own control, but it is the Universe which that decides and guides us. It is constantly moving us along many different paths. They eventually become clearer and showing us more for what are the right reasons. The reasoning may not always be clear, it is a case of accepting what is and what will be. Being open and looking at all situations with a balanced view. It all encompasses our journey, a journey to do with the discovery of ourselves. Keep doing what you do and moving forward. With good intention, your hopes and dreams kept alive and firmly at the forefront of your mind. Constantly undertake research, continue to learn, develop new skills, expand your thoughts and ideas. Ensure the fire burning inside stays alight and watch those embers spark into the brightest flames.

The time we have is totally precious
But so easily does it get wasted
We try doing something without success
The minutes and the hours tick by
In the end, it has beaten us
We many have not really achieved
The one thing we have really lost is time
Learning and trying are part of the test
That is part of the plan
We can and will try again
We do not admit or look at it as a defeat
It cannot always happen first time
Perseverance creates character
Shows fortitude and determination
A never give up or give in mental attitude
Keep trying, to keep going
Each time we learn something more about ourselves
It is all within our soul journey to learn
Accept today for what it has been
But be ready for that which is yet to come
Each day, an opportunity to develop.

Having strength to let go is important. It is as equally important as holding on. Yes, it may hurt to decide to let this happen, but it is important to know what to hold on to, what to keep, and that which is no longer of benefit. Always have belief and faith in your intuition to guide you. You will know the answer well before you decide. It will be tough, but it will be even tougher to stop this from happening. Have trust in yourself, forge your own path. If the rulebook is blocking you, throw away the book. We set rules for a reason, but they are not necessarily hard and fast for life. Find your own route, set an example. You may just find the direction that in time others will think yes, and then use themselves. Show that you can lead, not just one who always must follow. You always have choice, your own free will to find, choose, and take a different route. When you finally arrive at the designated destination, the encountered diversions will have enabled you to learn so much more along the way. Never hold yourself back, forget about any limitations, think unlimited. Your mind is a wonderfully powerful tool. Use it for your benefit, and for that of others.

The never-ending spiral, which is life
Going upwards, coming downwards
Which way do you see it?
This depends on your point of view
Either way, we take it one step at a time
We may not potentially be aware or see it happening
Each step being part of your soul journey
This lifetime forward once more, like all others
Consider and analyse occasionally where you have been
But also, think about where you are heading now
That is the conundrum
It is beyond us to always easily fully figure it all out
Accepting and trying to understand
Understanding can be the hardest part
Piecing it together is potentially impossible
Life is a possibility of endless possibilities
Such an enigma which we may never decode
Each having our own unique journey
Interlinking with many along the way
Sharing existence and endeavouring to understand Enjoy living it, however complex the true meaning.

Truly believing in who you are, in your own ability to cope, to overcome obstacles, that those mountains which lie ahead are only symbolic impediments. To have complete belief and faith that, however hard it may get, that it will eventually work. Keep doing, keep trying, keep being true to yourself. Yes, it may well get hard. It may be tougher than you could ever have imagined. Life is an unending challenge. Every day, something different occurs, but you try, and you persevere. Just be happy being you. Do not let those who elicit negative comments pull you down, away, and off from your chosen course. They are not you; they cannot be you, keep your head held high, your values sound, and have that belief in yourself that you will prevail. That staunch belief is about the belief in believing in yourself, because if you cannot, then how can you ever expect anyone else to? It starts with you and eventually ends with you.

Piece by piece by piece
Life is an eternal jigsaw
A multi complex three-dimensional puzzle
Which piece to look out for first
The outer edges potentially yes
But they keep us enclosed
One missing piece leaves a gap
Enables and allows escapement
Walls either visible or invisible
Moving beyond them
Free yourself willingly
Flying and finding your freedom
Inside us all there is a captured bird
We cannot see the wings
But they are there ready
Open them widely
Take that flight into the unknown
Fly and find your own world
Your yet imagined future
Fly high and keeping flying
Is it a flight of fantasy?
Maybe it is, but that matters not
It is all within your own reality.

Our souls will search for their counterpart endlessly. A journey which may take forever or could just happen. Eventually, they will hopefully find each other, and be back together. Although we always hope that this will occur within what we experience our human lifetime, this may not be the case. It is a journey beyond all known journeys. On occasions, we may think that we are close, only for disillusionment to reoccur and rear its head. We will constantly search and continue searching repeatedly. Even if we find neither our soulmate nor twin-flame, it does not mean that we have failed. It enables the search to continue onwards, into another period of both time and space. Our souls have an endless journey, and infinite opportunities to find each other more than once. So, never lose hope, just keep your belief with you, and have faith in yourself and the Universe.

We all naturally judge

Judgemental of others and always of ourselves

We are never good enough

Easy to put ourselves down

Others have so much more than we do

In the end, material things really do not matter

We come with nothing and leave with nothing

What does matter is how we treat each other

How we show respect, care, and kindness

How we give compassion, loyalty and love

These are of far greater importance

They are natural spiritual gifts and available freely

Truly meaningful and flowing through you as part of life

They are within the essence of your soul

Let yourself give these in abundance

Concentrate on living a life of inspired vision

Believing fully in yourself and in who you are

Trusting in the process of life, and abundant love

Forget about judging either yourself or others

Leave that thought process and the negativity it engenders.

Here is an interesting thought and not just for today: does our life have to have a grand plan and purpose, or is just muddling through and finding interesting things to do to fill out time sufficient? Surely, even just finding interesting things to do must have a purpose, because otherwise why would we even consider looking for these things to do or learn something new? What is a grand plan, anyway? We are all here for a specific reason, which has nothing to do with ambition. We can all succeed and be successful as the individuals which we are. But remember, life is about living, enjoyment, being happy, sharing kindness, and care. So whatever route you choose is the route that was pre-planned for you. Nothing, however small, is accidental. We may or may never know what that reason is. All we call do is accept the course we follow, and if it takes an entire lifetime to find out why, then we just must accept that is our course. Everyone has a different answer hidden within their journey. We can help each other learn and grow, but we cannot find their course, and they cannot find yours. Think about this often, with acceptance and understanding.

When you are down, nothing else seems to matter
You feel sad, forlorn and lost
Thoughts play on the mind like leaves in the wind
You try to find out, but there seems no reason
You wonder if there is an actual answer
Why has life treated you this way?
What have you done wrong?
Does it relate to this life or even to one in the past?
You constantly search for that needle in the haystack and a solution
Thoughts go round and round and round again
Constant longing without ever really knowing
Will you ever get to know?
Is it just a case of allowing yourself to let go?
To let get of that which serves no purpose
So many unanswered questions
That question itself becomes a puzzle
Potentially, there is an answer is out there
But you just must keep believing and having trust
Lift your spirits stay constantly connected to yourself
Firmly believing there is a solution, and you will find it.

Stress levels can be high even on those days when everything seems to go well, something suddenly can occur which causes a complete unbalance. What we need to do is try ensuring that we do not let that unexpected stress affect us. Yes, this is difficult. Trying to stay balanced is the best you can in order and to keep the storm away. Without knowing it, you may have been used and manipulated so much that you do not know where you are, or even what you are doing. Situations that take you to places well beyond your thought control. Without stress, the storm does not and cannot exist. This is all easier said than done. Just keep trying your hardest, and whatever the circumstances, endeavour to stay calm, focused, and in control. You have the power of control over your thoughts and actions. Have that inbuilt strength to rise above situations. Conflict is never easily controllable or avoided. Just try your best to find an opportunity for logical judgement, rather than direct action. A solution is in theory only a thought away.

Life is so extremely fragile
We are all mortal and only here for a time
Do we know what will happen tomorrow?
Or even the day after?
In fact, do we know what will happen in the next few minutes?
No, of course not
We hope it will be nothing serious
It is what makes life the mystery which it is
Uncertainty mixed with a sense sometimes of insecurity
Remembering that each minute which passes is precious
They go so quickly, and most are unnoticeable
We need to try the best we can to appreciate them all
Sadly, life constantly impedes so much
All we can do is what we can do
Make time to reflect, realise, and contemplate
Live your life, do not let it drift endlessly by
It is yours; it is for living, not for losing
We are as fragile as life itself.

Today, once again like yesterday, we will have many distinct moments which can change suddenly and without warning. It is an ongoing test; constantly questioning and examining our resolve. Life easily becomes stretched to the limit, but we overcome these daily obstacles. We have more strength and fortitude than initially meets the eye, pushing as far as is it is possible, even further than is potentially necessary. Testing themselves against themselves, time and time again. A battle of endeavour, of endurance, of deep embedded character, showing that they can rise to challenges. Obstacles, both seen and unseen, which are way beyond the norm. They are not super humans; they are human, just like all of us. What stands them apart is that they want to do it because they can and have the willpower to do it. If we put our minds to it, we can all achieve so much more than we do. It is so easy to live within what is our comfort zone, but unless we try, we never ever will know the limit to which we can go. Just focus on yourself and use the ability you have. You will amaze yourself when you take that leap of faith. It can be done; you can do it.

Each day we start our journey again
We start it off afresh once again
Trying our absolute hardest
To do our everything that we can
Keeping motivated and staying strong
But never forgetting to show kindness
Naturally, give kindness to all others
Plus kindness for yourself and more care for all
It is free and such a simple choice to make
Less judging of what others do or think
Leaving the need to worry about any nonessentials
Staying focused and true to yourself
Show your faithfulness, honesty, love, and loyalty
It is straightforward and meaningful
Practice this philosophy every day
Make it an automatic part of your daily routine
Today, tomorrow and always there afterwards.

Each single future step we take will be different. They cannot be the same, however similar they may feel.

We continually move forwards with the Universe listening to our wants and needs. Allow time for it to happen because it will respond in its own time. It is infinitely unlimited working within its own timescale, which may not correspond with yours. It is natural to want everything to happen immediately in the here and now. This cannot be the case. Wait and be true to yourself. Always show gratitude, rise above issues that do not serve. Whatever occurs, whatever happens, life continues and goes on. Changes happen which result in it never being quite the same again. This is something that we must accept and to learn and to live with. The learning curve, which is life, is constantly onwards and upwards. Show your benevolence and understanding that you only want the share which is yours. That which is there waiting for you. Waiting for you, in the relevant place, and at the right time.

The way forward is out there
It is somewhere within your future
Just keeping looking and searching
Many varying obstacles and paths await
Find them and the journey which each will entail
Experiences help us develop and grow
We can all enable this as part of our reality
Although nothing is ever certain
New doors and future opportunities await
Believe that anything and everything is possible
Whilst staying focused, remain constantly hopeful
Continually show your appreciation and gratitude
Like a magnet, what we give, we receive in return
The force becomes more intense and forever stronger
As our development continues and life progresses
The purpose for us being here materialises
We continually learn about ourselves
Life is a forever learning and never-ending lesson
So never presume that there is nothing more to learn
Keep your focus always
Opportunities will appear from nowhere.

Even when experiencing the most difficult of days, with more lows than highs, there is still so much to be thankful for. The circle of life continually revolves around a never-ending rollercoaster journey of difficulties. Never knowingly exactly what each day may bring, we constantly need to stay aware, accept all situations, and continually look forward. Having eager anticipation of what can and may often unexpectedly occur, either to your benefit or disadvantage. The future is not some distant date many years away from now. The future is happening now as we think and speak. If we wait, then we miss those opportunities which are there every day. The art is to spot the ones which will be beneficial and leave well alone those which are not helpful. Enjoy today and keep saying to yourself that better times are awaiting ahead. I am ready and coming to get them.

We are here as we are for now
Our spirit having taken on human form
Experiencing this time and passing through
The time we get here is but limited
So, it is essential to learn and make the most of it
How long we get, that is so difficult to tell
We have all come for a specific reason
Knowingly unknown and gradually experiencing
Different paths take us onwards
This is an entirely different dimension
We experience creation
The test of what living this life means
Remembering that as one door closes, another becomes open
Whilst here, ensure you choose the best options for you
This is but a fleeting moment in time and space
Develop and use your imagination
Live your life, never lose or waste your life
It is your life and yours alone
Never worry about what others think
They are not you and never can be.

It is such a privilege to be reborn each new day. We take this and life for granted, but life is precious, and enjoying every moment as much as we can is so important. To live, love, laugh. To be happy, kind, caring, grateful, and gracious. Look after your family, your friends, your nearest and dearest, and include yourself too. You are just as important as everyone else. Looking after your physical and mental health is so important to your own wellbeing. Times of stress and uncertainty happen to us all, and unknowingly, you might suffer with one or even both. Make sure that you look after your body, mind, and spirit. Take time out for you, when needed. If you need to do nothing, then do nothing. There is nothing wrong with taking time out. Nurture and give yourself unconditional kindness and gentle, loving care. Because if you do not, you cannot expect anyone else to do this for you. You are important, realise this. It is essential to make yourself a priority.

Life should be a joyous experience
The bigger picture potentially unseen
There may not always be a second chance
Ensure you are ready and prepared
First impressions are important and matter
They can make the difference
So, make sure of being composed
Stand up and make yourself count
Be resourceful, strong, even authoritative
Tall, alert, purposeful and ready
You have natural, inbuilt wisdom
Guile, aptitude and strength
Use these skills wisely
Understand that timing is important
It lapses and eventually runs out
We are continually moving forwards
Life is a multifaceted and complex
But potentially a fun experience
Miracles happen daily
They may only be minor ones
But be open to seeing them
They occur everywhere
The art is spotting them
Allow them to help you, enjoy your life.

Your mindset plays such an important part in your day-to-day world, helping to keep thoughts flowing. Enabling your positivity throughout the day to stay focused. You are the controller; it is totally up to you. Endeavour, however hard it may be, to stay balanced with your thoughts, emotions, feelings, and reactions at every moment. Doing this will gradually help change your entire thought process and mental attitude. Today is an ideal day and opportunity to do something that your future self will be proud of. Do not wait until tomorrow. That philosophy deals with delay. Start that building process step-by-step today. You will be thankful that you did. So, start the process now without procrastination and leave those areas of negativity in your past. Focus on the here, and on the now. Make it happen today, and a day you remember well in the progression of your future journey.

Remember to always let things go
Do not let negative issues linger
Those nagging harmful thoughts
They develop and grow into situations
They become problematic
Draining not just you but others
Forget about them completely
What has happened has happened
It is now gone and is in the past
Start again with a clean slate
With a loving heart that is ready
Let your mind be clear
Remove unnecessary, wasteful clutter
Let go for good of that which is gone
It serves no meaningful purpose
Move forward purposefully
Stay focused attentive resolute
You are far more than you imagine
It is your time to develop and grow.

We may all appear similar, but it is our soul knowledge and journey which is different. Our journeys are all developing separately, but for many unknown reasons, our paths have crossed so that we learn lessons from one another. Putting this into simple layperson's terms, we are all different, but have a common goal in raising our spiritual vibrations and development. To help each of us move forwards. Remember that taking time to be quiet each day is important, and a necessary element of who you are becoming. You can do this first thing in the morning, or at a convenient moment during the day, even if it needs to be the last thing at night. You do not have to do it at the same time each day. It is up to you to choose the time and place. The main thing, though, is to do it. The more you do it, the easier it becomes, and stronger the connection. Find time for yourself to do this, and let yourself get to know yourself better.

Do we always see everything clearly?
Are we looking unfocused at the situation?
Is it a case of what the eye does not see
Sometimes we need to look beyond the obvious
A change of our own perspective
Allowing us to see, accept, and fully understand
If you focus on the space there within
The place there deep in your mind
When you are perfectly still and quiet,
You will find many unanswered questions
The mind can take you anywhere
Back to your past, or into the unseen future
Such unused and untapped power
Into the dimension which is all your own
Allow yourself this journey often
It is something to make alone
An encounter with yourself
An opportunity of discovery
So, go within travel and find those answers
To an infinite number of questions
Questions that have been there waiting
What you find will help shape your future.

Everything comes, goes and passes in its own time. We very often have not the control over where we go, who we meet, or how our life will take shape. It is therefore important to always expect the unexpected, allow the pieces to fall into place, and accept that which occurs as having meant to be. Sometimes the more we want something to happen, the more we push, the harder it becomes, and the further away it ends up from being where or what we want. Allowance is important, to breathe, relax and realise that most of life is well beyond our control. Survival and taking each day one at a time enables focus. Looking too far forward can simply bring anxiety. We then we become anxious, wanting life to move along at a speed we can control. We only have control over ourselves, not life completely. Reality moves at its own pace, it goes its own direction, in its own time. Once we accept this concept, we can then realise that acceptance is far more important than expectation.

Mother Earth

Father Sky

Our planet needs realignment

Earthquakes

Volcano eruptions

Tsunamis, and unrelenting storms

You try to find balance

We need to find a plan

What comes next?

A plague, floods, drought

Never ending shortages

Famine, fire, damnation, pestilence

Society is struggling

Turmoil is coming

It is an issue growing worse daily

We are now within a constant conflict

A battle with ourselves and within humanity

The battle for survival has started

Our saviour is us and we can survive

But the potential apocalypse is upon us

The end, or a new era beginning, beckons

Life as we knew, it will not be the life we know

But it can be better with understanding

Our planet is drifting out of alignment

It is not too late to fix, if we all work together

Find balance and realise the importance

Planning, for us, our children, and their children, too.

We all are part of the same world and within the one universe. All having our own place within it where we currently live. Just try to remember the importance of this each morning. We are all blessed having this opportunity. Also, remember that you are an amazingly unique individual. There is only one of you. Others may sadly make derogatory judging comments, ignore them and just remember who you are. You are special, always will be special. Not just to yourself, as there will no doubt also be someone somewhere to whom you will be just as special. Forget thoughts of any failings or foibles, rise above unnecessary and painful comment and criticism. If you want to change, then do that simply and solely for you and only for you. You are you. They are not you, they never will or can ever be you. Keep a positive attitude throughout each day and practice this daily.

I stand on the edge of the cliff
The ocean pounds relentlessly below
This jump will take all my courage
It will take everything I could ever believe
The waves smash against the rocks
I tense and look at the sky
My silent prayer bounces in my mind
I breathe deeply, and then take another deep breath
I ready myself and feel my muscles tighten
I leap high and into the unknown
Flying first then, crashing downwards
Taking what seems like forever
I hit the water with unbelievable force
Down downwards, I go
Into the icy depth and darkness
Struggling now to resurface
I see a glimpse of light and know I am saved
Finally, I breathe in clean, wonderfully fresh air
Life already feels different
Just as if I have been reborn
Was it a dream or my reality?
It matters not because each day rebirth occurs.

What are your thoughts on enlightenment? Is it all we imagine it might be, a mystical–magical place that one day we will find when exploring the world? This is highly unlikely, and very much a misconception. It has absolutely nothing to do with what we think or imagine. It is to do with us individually, personally, enabling us to break down those barriers, those walls of doubt which have encroached on our soul. During our many journeys, we will have been through turmoil, through torment, through mental torture, time after time. We have survived, learnt, developed, because our soul knows who we always are. It has protected us, and always will. Having seen us rise; and having seen us fall; it will have seen us rise again. Within those moments of wonder, it is when we find something new about ourselves. Something that we did not know about, finding the authentic you. It will help to awaken that aspect of your soul, the part which was there, but always just hidden. This manifestation may or may not happen fully within this lifetime. As our journey is endless, we should have no expectation or presumption of when it may occur. Continuing to accept, to allow, to learn, we enable what will be to happen within our life plan.

I reached deep inside myself
I pulled away that no which no longer served
I felt myself open and feel new
A doorway invisible to the eye
It had always been waiting
Even I had no clue it was there
Deep within, hidden all my life
A part of who I always was now emerging
A fragmented part of myself
I never knew that it existed
We all have something extra to find
We never need a key, as there is no physical lock
There is no actual handle to turn
It is a metaphysical concept
Somewhere between mind, body, and spirit
Finding your this genuine connection
Releases your own magic
Opening new ideas and different thoughts
Enabling a change of life, of direction
If I can do it, and I have
You can do it too, and hopefully you will.

Peacefully enthusiastic, inspiringly motivated, but approachable and considerate. This surely must be how we all want to be, and want to be treated? It is easy. It just needs that realisation that we are here to help one another. To learn and to grow off each other. The teacher pupil scenario works both ways, and we can be both at the same time. Giving guidance, but also being open. Accepting new methods, thoughts, and ideas. Not sticking to a dogmatic principle, of always being right or knowing best. Being ready to accept that perhaps you may not know best. Having a flexible and open-minded attitude. Living life this way is relatively straightforward and easy. It may need perseverance, but with patience, you will edge nearer to excellence. We will never reach perfection, but that should never mean ever stopping or trying. Stay true to yourself. Maintain adaptability always.

It was so dark
Darker than the darkest night
Not one speck of light
It was scary and the inside unknowing
I stepped through the entrance portal
I ventured slowly forwards
Feeling my way as I went
I could sense things were close to hand
My footsteps echoed with my heartbeat
Anticipation gripped me from within
Suddenly I heard a whispered voice
It seemed to say my name
The voice was calming
It was reassuring
It seemed so familiar
I realised it was my voice
It was telling me not to panic
Deeper and deeper I went
I stayed focused, stayed positive
Suddenly, a tiny orb of light appeared
It came from nowhere
Then another and they joined with others
All floating as a mass around me
I knew then that I was finding myself
The darkness was it in my imagination
Was this just a vivid dream?
Reality had never seemed so real
Either way, fear had gone, and I felt alive